Copyright © 2013 by Murali Murthy

First Edition – November 2013

ISBN

978-1-4602-3068-8 (Hardcover)

978-1-4602-3069-5 (Paperback)

978-1-4602-3070-1 (eBook)

All rights reserved.

No part of this publication may be reproduced in any form, or by any means, electronic or mechanical, including photocopying, recording, or any information browsing, storage, or retrieval system, without permission in writing from the publisher.

Produced by:

FriesenPress

Suite 300 – 852 Fort Street

Victoria, BC, Canada V8W 1H8

www.friesenpress.com

Distributed to the trade by The Ingram Book Company.

"Mountains are not stadiums where I satisfy my ambition to achieve, they are the cathedrals where I practice my religion...I go to them as humans go to worship. From their lofty summits I view my past, dream of the future and, with an unusual acuity, am allowed to experience the present moment...my vision cleared, my strength renewed. In the mountains I celebrate creation. On each journey I am reborn."

Anatoli Boukreev

Table of Contents

Also by Murali Murthy

"The ACE Principle works. Follow the guidelines Murali Murthy has set out and you'll become a success magnet."

Raymond Aaron - NY Times best-selling author, Founder, Raymond Aaron Group, www.Aaron.com

"This book is loaded with practical ideas to educate, motivate and inspire you to set and achieve bigger goals than ever before."

Brian Tracy - Professional Speaker, best-selling author, "Earn what you're really worth" entrepreneur and success expert, www.BrianTracy.com

Praise for *The ACE Awakening*

"Murali's second book in The ACE Series, The ACE Awakening offers a rare insight into the challenges we must all confront and triumph, with the assured self-knowledge that only comes from pushing life to its extremes.

The ACE Awakening reverberates right from the get-go with an inviting, inspiring cover, daring the reader to awaken the greatness within. Well-written and easy flowing, the eight chapters in the book, appropriately titled Milestones, are still comprehensive in scope and encompass the journey of perseverance and resilience as the author traverses across five mountains.

Murali is an accomplished author with the specific expertise to make this book the great treatise that it is. His writing style is direct and ferociously honest, while his use of emotionally gripping anecdotes infuses an engaging, novelistic feel. The ACE Awakening is a gripping must-read."

Ruben Gonzalez - *"The Olympic Speaker"*, Four-time Olympian, Award-winning Speaker, Highly Acclaimed Business Author, Co-star of the Personal Development movie *Pass It On*, www.OlympicMotivation.com

"Murali Murthy has written the book that almost every coach, motivator, counselor etc. will read and wish that THEY had written! Many books today are long on motivation, but fall short of providing the actual action steps required to get out there and make something happen.

The ACE Awakening is extremely well balanced and will not only stir something deep inside of you but will show you what to do with those feelings!"

Vincent Harris, M.S. - Body Language Expert and Author of *The Productivity Epiphany,* www.VinceHarris.com

"The ACE Awakening is a must read for those who are serious about their success! Read it and Get Ready To Grow!"

Dr. Willie Jolley - CSP, CPAE (Member-Speaker Hall of Fame), Best Selling Author *A Setback Is A Setup For A Comeback!,* www.WillieJolley.com

"The ACE Awakening takes Murali Murthy's journey to a new level. He shares his insights and experiences on the journey and lessons learned and how impactful and memorable the destination can be. A magical book read that will inspire you to achieve your goals."

Jim Pagiamtzis - Published Author, Speaker and Entrepreneur, Founder of 21 Connections, www.21connections.ca

"Everyone has mountains to climb. Load your backpack and follow Murali's advice on how to Absorb, Comprehend and Excel while climbing your mountain to success."

David Cottrell - Author of *Monday Morning Leadership, Tuesday Morning Coaching and Indispensable!,* www.CornerStoneLeadership.com

"Take your time absorbing The ACE Awakening. Open your mind and let the chapters sink in. And actively participate in the ACE Insights to build the destiny you were meant to live."

Jeffrey J. Fox - Bestselling author of *How to Become CEO, How to Be a Fierce Competitor* and *How to Become a Rainmaker,* www.foxandcompany.com

"The ACE Awakening is a valuable step by step guide to work through your life in a meaningful way. It acknowledges that life is not meant to be easy, but rather that we can be at ease with its difficulties and learn from them. Deeply spiritual,

this guide will intrigue and challenge you regardless of your faith or beliefs. Your journey awaits!"

Rod Macdonald - International Fitness Expert and Speaker, Best-selling Author of *Total Fat Destruction* and Co-Author of *Foundations of Professional Personal Training.* www.totalfatdestruction.com

"Murali Murthy's new book encourages readers to commit to their passions with discipline, patience, and perseverance. The easy routes in life are all circular, burrowing ones. The ACE Awakening teaches us that inspiring vistas will be found only on uphill paths of tenacious effort."

Bruce S. Garrabrandt - Best-selling Author, *The Power of Having Desire* and *Make Yourself Ageless,* http://www.artbybruce.com

"We all face "mountains to climb" and many give up before they begin. The challenge is to push forward; either go over it, under it, thru it, around it, but make sure you conquer it. Murali Murthy's newest book The ACE Awakening is a no-nonsense mountain climber's dream. Buy this book, read this book, use its principles and conquer those mountains in your life."

Dr. Peter Legge - OBC, CSP, CPAE, HoF, Author, Professional Speaker, Businessman

"Murali's latest book is written in a friendly, easy to read style, giving readers a first hand account of his personal journey climbing the five peaks of Sabarimala and the challenges he faced crossing this difficult and unfriendly terrain. Most importantly, it contains practical, useable advice and actionable ideas, based on his own strategies for overcoming those seemingly insurmountable challenges"

Jim Donovan - best-selling author of *What are you waiting for? It's Your Life,* www.JimDonovan.com

"Murthy, the creator of The ACE Principle now gives us tools for an ACE Awakening: those that will help us absorb and comprehend life lessons in order to excel in whatever endeavor we tackle. From its first pages, The ACE Awakening lets us know how different it is from other titles on the shelves.

Instead of chapter names, the table of contents in Murthy's new book lists "milestones," starting with identifying our life purpose and ending with the one at which we reach the peak of the proverbial mountain. With Murthy's guidance, we, too, can enjoy the spectacular view from the top."

Marshall Goldsmith - 2 million-selling author, editor of 34 books, including the New York Times bestsellers, *MOJO* and *What Got You Here Won't Get You There*, www.marshallgoldsmithlibrary.com

Dedication

To the innumerable Swamis from around the world who join me on the truly unique trek of Sabarimala each year.

Thank you for helping me stretch in many ways so I can scale the five mighty peaks and successfully reach the summit each year.

Thank you for empowering me to be able to scale every mountain of my journey, each day of my life.

Acknowledgments

It is often said that you don't find a book to write, the book finds you. This book brought its own purpose and I merely followed its lead.

In chronicling my life experiences for over 26 years, one experience has led to another, one person to another, and so the story unfolded. The realization of this book has been a long journey much like the story of the trek itself and I could not have crossed the many milestones in accomplishing this journey without the exceptional support and guidance of the following people.

My deep sense of gratitude to Shri H. Nagaraj, author of *All About Sabarimala Ayyappa*, and Shri Aravind Subramanyam, author of *Nothing But Ayyappa*, for their factual accounts and rich detail on the entire Sabarimala experience.

As always, I am indebted to Myrna Riback, my ever vigilant and worldly-wise editor, who ensured that I never strayed off track while relating my story. Her invaluable life insights and rare wisdom that come only with experience, her many suggestions and patient revisions are the reason you are holding the book in your hands in this form now.

And, of course, my huge thanks to the folks on **The ACE** team - Where would I be without you all?

Shalu my wife, for her strict, watchful eye in scrutinizing everything from the design of the cover, to the structure of the content, to the size of the fonts.

Manish Jetly for his able web and marketing support and constant source of inspiration.

Avinash Sonone, Mohammed Abdul Majeed, Nikhil Wad and Vaisakh KV, the exceptional team of Art Directors for lending this book the touch of elegance from the cover to the pages inside.

Tim Lindsay and Ceilidh Marlow, the Friesen Press team for their continued belief and unflinching support.

And, finally, to my mentor Nick Noorani who, for the second time, planted the idea for a book in me. Thanks, Nick, for persuading me to open up and pen my life story - something that I had been hesitant and shy to do for over 26 years.

To Shalu, Nick and all the above, and to you, dear reader, this book is a tribute to your faith in me.

Foreword

Mountain climbing has always been the best parallel analogy for success in life. From the earliest point in recorded history, human beings wanted to stand on the top of the world. As someone interested in human achievement and motivating people through my books, speeches, columns, and movies, I have read dozens of books about mountain climbing.

As a blind person myself and the author of 25 books, it is embarrassing for me to admit that when I could read with my eyes as most of the millions of people around the world read my books, I don't know that I ever read a full book cover to cover. After losing my sight, thanks to the National Library for the Blind and high-speed audio books, I consume an entire book virtually every day. This has opened my world in wonderful ways.

I remember reading Dick Bass' and Frank Wells' accounts of climbing the Seven Summits – which are the tallest peaks on each of the continents. In their book, they told great stories of their epic adventure throughout that year, but they really never offered their readers advice on how their mountaintop experience could impact people in their personal and professional lives.

In this book, Murali Murthy will use the experience of mountain climbing not as the entire story, but as a platform from which to examine your life and your goals. Never take advice from anyone who doesn't have what you want. The author you will meet in these pages has not only climbed literal mountains, but has helped other people climb the virtual mountains we all face in our lives.

I have had four of my novels turned into major motion pictures. One of my movie partners is fond of saying, "If you can tell a good story, you earn the right to share your message." Murali Murthy has been to the mountaintop and deserves your and my attention as we focus on our own lives today and into the future. I hope you will not only read carefully and enjoy, but I hope the lessons in this book will help you reach new mountaintops in your own life.

Jim Stovall - World Renowned Speaker and Author of the best-selling book, *The Ultimate Gift,* now a 20th Century Fox major motion picture. He is Founder and President of the Emmy Award-winning Narrative Television Network. www. jimstovall.com

"Success is not counted by how high you have climbed but by how many people you brought with you."

Will Rose

Introduction

What keeps you humble and human?

This is the question I ask myself from time to time. It is often easy to become complacent with where we are and preoccupied with what we have achieved in life. And if we are not watchful, we may begin to feel smug. And that is why I try to put myself on auto correction every time there seems to be a slight dip, deviation or indifference.

I am an active student of personal development and if there is one thing that I have learned from some of my truly successful heroes, it is that they all have systems in place to ensure they continue to grow and remain strong. More importantly, perhaps, these systems are able to help them stay humble even at the height of their achievements.

The mountains I climbed in my twenties made me the strong person I am today. While mountains are always hard to climb, I have gotten more skillful over the years and the climbing part has gotten easier. The many things that I have learned on each of my climbing expeditions have given me, and continue to give me, a grateful heart and a humble outlook.

Your mountain may not be made of stone; it may be striving to improve an important relationship, balancing your finances, fulfilling a dream of travelling the world or proving a theorem no one thought possible.

What climbing towards any goal has in common with climbing a mountain is that they are all amazing experiences. Whatever it is, it pushes you beyond your limits, beyond what you ever thought you could do. And, in the end, it shows you how much you really can do and what you really are capable of.

What mountain peak do you wish to scale?
How will you reach your Pinnacle of Excellence?

I invite you to experience *The ACE Awakening.*

Decide what you want to change, what you wish to improve or what you yearn to accomplish. Choose to focus in positive and fully connected ways.
Act on your Awakening.
Reach your Pinnacle.

Murali Murthy

"The unexamined life is not worth living."

Socrates

The ACE Connection

Why did I call this book *The ACE Awakening?* Why not just *The Awakening*?

How did my personal mountain climbing experiences awaken my need to write the ACE books? And what is ACE anyway?

The ACE Principle does the following:
It calls upon the readers to **ABSORB**.
It then allows them to **COMPREHEND**.
It offers suggestions to **EXCEL**.

Our lives are the result of what we observe, how we interpret and how we apply that information each moment. What we ABSORB and how we COMPREHEND are critical to how we EXCEL. I wrote my first book, *The ACE Principle* to help people learn how to Absorb, Comprehend and Excel in every area of their lives.

The ACE Principle, made up of 15 Success Principles, serves as a reliable handbook to help the reader discover the answers himself - a handy reference always at the ready to help him make the right choices.

My quest for self improvement and personal growth is constant. It means I'm always looking for ways to increase my capacity to grow, develop and achieve more. Once I had completed T*he Ace Principle,* I started to become more introspective, and was then inspired to write *The ACE Awakening*, a book that would show my own journey towards personal growth and achievement by chronicling an important part of my life story, arduous mountain climbing.

All good stories have a beginning, a middle and an end. A good story will introduce a conflict that draws the reader in and challenges him and, then, provides resolutions to the conflicts that go beyond the page to the benefit of the reader too. *The ACE Awakening* allows the reader to observe the issues I face, the personal challenges I experience and how I prevail to achieve the successful outcome that I aspire to. It is my hope that my story will inspire others to reach for excellence as well.

Thus, it was the 'awakening' within me that first led me to formulate The ACE Principles. Just as all the major experiences in your life can lead you to formulate the ways to achieve the pinnacle of your life.

I hope that through *The ACE Principle* and through this book, *The Ace Awakening,* you will discover your own awakening that will help you probe some of the struggles in your own lives, clearly identify solutions and experience meaningful success.

To you, dear reader, I offer this humble gift - *The ACE Awakening.*

"One does not climb to attain enlightenment, rather one climbs because he is enlightened."

Zen Master Futomaki

The Inspiration

Climbing a mountain.

Each year, I trek over 60 kilometres across one the most inhospitable terrains in Southern India and join thousands of people from around the world who overcome extreme challenges to climb five peaks in the attempt to reach the Summit of Sabarimala.

As I write this book, I have successfully climbed Sabarimala 26 years in a row.

Why did I want to climb a mountain?

On my very first trip to Sabarimala, that question was answered. Because mountains are majestic and inspire awe. They tower and loom above us. They outscale us. When we climb a mountain, we participate in its majesty and awe. Some part of its aura enters our life story and imbues it with meaning. It is not that we become as great as the mountain when we scale it but, rather, its greatness becomes part of us. That power which loomed over us at the foot goes inside us at the peak.

Sabarimala: Sabarimala or Mount Sabari rises 3000 feet above sea level and lies in the Sahyadris, the Western Ghats in India. It is the site of one of the largest annual pilgrimages in the world with an estimated 50–60 million devotees walking barefoot through forests abounding in wildlife as they climb to the summit.

After all these years, this extraordinary experience still helps me appreciate the wonderful gift of life, revel in the humanity of my fellow man and, above all, stay grounded and humble.

By accomplishing something that was so beyond what I thought I was capable of, my belief system had no choice but to change radically.

Climbing a mountain showed me that massive accomplishment equals massive confidence.

When you accomplish a bold and daring goal, your belief in who you are and what you are capable of shifts in almost direct proportion to the size of the goal. Today I have confidence in who I am and what I can accomplish.

MILESTONE

Identifying a Life Purpose

Challenge is the core and mainspring of all human activity.
If there's an ocean, we cross it; if there's a disease, we cure it;
if there's a wrong, we right it; if there's a record, we break it;
and, finally, if there's a mountain, we climb it".

James Ramsey Ullman

Discover what you are good at, what you love to do that gives your life meaning. Once you know what it is, pursue it.

Why climb a mountain?

To restore a sense of meaning in your life.

The climb reminds you of the significance of life. It reveals that, in the context of a vast universe, there is still immense untapped power within each of us. That power, even in the face of the greater power of the mountain before us, is not insignificant.

Perhaps most importantly, climbing Sabarimala helped me build the confidence to embark on a personal journey to reach my own personal Pinnacle of Excellence.

Ayyappa is one of the many Hindu Gods of India whose worship is more prevalent in the southern part of the country. Among other things, the Ayyappa legend is famous for its temple at the summit of Sabarimala which is open to people from all castes, creeds, religions, social status or nationality. Each year, millions of people from around the world trek to the summit of the mountain to pay their obeisance. Today, the pilgrims comprise every religion, though mostly Hindu, Christian and Muslim. It is a spiritual journey that underscores universal brotherhood, regardless of caste and creed.

When I was 17, I was diagnosed with a malignant tumour and my parents admitted me to a private hospital in the Anna Nagar West suburb of Chennai, India.

I was operated on and stayed at the hospital for approximately a week. After the operation, I was transferred to a room on the third floor from whose window I could see an Ayyappa Temple right across the road.

Until then, I would not have considered myself a spiritual person in any sense but, that day, as I looked out of the window, I found myself promising myself that, if I was cured, the first thing I would do when I was discharged would be to come and offer my prayers and express gratitude for my health.

The day they discharged me, I stepped out of the hospital and walked across the street. For the first time in my life, I consciously stepped into an Ayyappa Temple.

At that moment, precisely 9 o'clock in the morning, I made a promise in the Ayyappa Temple.

I declared: "I will climb the mountain of Sabarimala."

I had never climbed a mountain before, not even a small one.

But, suddenly, the mountain called to me and the act of climbing it became something I had to do. It had begun as a symbolic gesture but had somehow assumed a higher importance. Something inside me needed it.

There I was, all of 17 years old, in the exuberance of youth and suddenly there was the mountain. I felt overwhelmed and yet significant at the same time. Somehow that relationship of power and powerlessness spoke to me like nothing before.

I have never regretted the decision I made that eventful day. In fact, I grow stronger each year and my life mission becomes clearer with each passing year.

ACE *Insights*

1

Reach Your Pinnacle of Excellence

Each year, climbing Sabarimala helps me embark on a personal journey to reach my Pinnacle of Excellence.

I believe that the journey to the Pinnacle is, at its heart, a relentless determination to develop and improve ourselves to the highest degree possible.

This journey starts with a foundation of strong belief in oneself and the conviction that we are stronger than we think and we can accomplish amazing things.

This determination presents itself in several ways:

- A willingness to reflect upon and strengthen your personality, actions and thoughts.
- A desire to improve your life each day, each moment.
- An eagerness to seek out challenges.
- A desire to learn as many new skills as possible.
- A desire to hone, refine and master the skills you already possess.
- A willingness to endure discomfort, uncertainty and pain in the pursuit of improvement.

We can cultivate the mindset to heighten our determination. Begin with the willingness to take on personal challenges on a small scale. In this way, you can develop the strong decision-making skills needed to weather much bigger challenges.

We reach the Pinnacle of Excellence by taking one step at a time, focusing fully on the immediate step in front of us and performing to our fullest potential.

The 3 spokes on the wheel that take me to my Pinnacle of Excellence are:

1. Stretching My Limits.
   Consistently working to perform closer to my potential.

2. Maximizing Life.
   Consciously striving to achieve more and be more.

3. Finding Peace Within.
   Energetically undertaking to live with more joy and harmony in life.

1. Stretching Your Limits – Work consistently to perform closer to your potential

Peak Point

Stay curious and always be learning.

If you are stagnant, you'll never learn to truly fly.

The human mind can perform 20,000 trillion calculations per second. But research shows we do not use more than 10% of our potential brain power.

Human beings are blessed with the capacity to appreciate a wide variety of experiences. We can explore the world and learn new things, experiment with our creativity, develop special relationships and change the circumstances of our environment.

Each of us has the power within us to create the life we want, the life we dream about, the life we were born to live. Each of us deserves to fulfill our full potential and manifest our true destiny. It is our birthright. But we must actively earn it through hard work. That hard work begins with first learning and then living by the time-tested and ageless principles that are guaranteed to bring about the desired results.

Our lives are revealed to us by the choices we make. If you honestly assess where you are with respect to your quality of life, you will see that you alone are responsible for where you are.

We are all fledglings, amateurs, when we begin. But, as we master an art we truly focus on, we become full of knowledge and capable of things that seem supernatural. That is the relentless pursuit of perfection.

2. Maximizing Life – Consciously striving to achieve more and be more

Peak Point

Don't see learning as a road to knowledge.

Let learning lead to action.

As you stretch to achieve more in life, the greater the access you gain to a vast variety of options. As you learn to change, grow and adapt, more opportunities come hurtling towards you.

One of my favorite ways to maximize life is to pack my bags and embark on a journey.

Travel opens my mind and exponentially introduces me to more possibilities for improvement.

Travel helps me reflect on the things I have already achieved and allows me the scope to ask myself questions about what is next. Travel gives me the opportunity to realign my priorities so my life can be in perfect harmony.

Travel gives me the space and time to reflect on my life and the distance to ask myself questions and be positively critical of things I want and need to change.

Make a list of things you would like to do to enhance your life so that, the next time you say to yourself, "When I have more time, I would like to." you can become aware of areas in your life that are not as fulfilling as you would like them to be.

This list will also give you a new perspective on how to channel your energy so that it can contribute more to your satisfaction of life and create a more satisfying balance and feeling of achievement.

In Social Interactions

- When was the last time you expressed appreciation to a co-worker?
- Have you taken advantage of opportunities to contribute to a committee?
- How active are you in your community and civic organizations?

In the Pleasures of Leisure

- What have you read recently that brings you joy?
- What was the last movie you saw that excited you?
- What was the last piece of music you heard that made you feel like dancing?

In Health and Fitness

- Is your chosen exercise program bringing you joy?
- Are you recognizing the benefits of stretching regularly?
- What foods are you eating on a regular basis to support good nutrition?

In Career and Finances

- What was the last activity or project that you really enjoyed spending time on?
- Each day, do you celebrate the progress you are making towards your career and business goals?
- Are you saving money on a regular basis to prepare for the future?
- Do you joyfully acknowledge the money that comes to you?
- What actions do you take to consistently manage money wisely?

In Relationships

- When was the last time you spent time with your closest friend?
- When was the last time you spent special time with family members?
- Was the experience fulfilling and joyful?

- If not, why wasn't it?
- What special experience did you share with your spouse in the last week?

In Spiritual Development

- When was the last time you meditated?
- When was the last time you sought out something to read that fed your spirit?
- When was the last time you spent time with others who share your spiritual beliefs?
- When was the last time you learned something new about someone else's spiritual beliefs?

3. Finding Peace Within – Undertaking to live with more joy and harmony in life

Peak Point

To discover yourself, lose yourself.

As our society grows more and more complex, finding true peace becomes more and more difficult. But we all need peace of mind to make important decisions, to help us get over traumas from our past and to deal with anxiety and frustration in our present lives.

If we cannot achieve a peaceful state then we are not balanced and we cannot achieve serenity. Peace of mind is a state that allows us to be the best people we can be and to live the full life that we were meant to live.

In order to achieve inner peace, you must embrace your beliefs. Do not let a busy lifestyle distract you and rob you off that wonderful feeling of inner calm for which your soul thirsts.

One thing we may all agree on is that having a solid, healthy faith is crucial because it is the guide that leads our conscience towards peace and wisdom. Research has shown that people who are deeply devoted to their faith have a higher life expectancy and are less likely to develop diseases such as cancer. This is because they experience more inner peace that helps them increase their quality of life.

Whatever you believe in, embrace it with your entire being. When you do, peace will find its way into your heart.

MILESTONE

2

The Insight and the Understanding

"When you ride your bike, you're working your legs, but your mind is on a treadmill. When you play chess, your mind is clicking along, but your body is stagnating. Climbing brings it together in a beautiful, magical way. The adrenaline is flowing, and it's flowing all the time."

Pat Ament

One of the reasons I think my vow to climb Sabarimala spoke so clearly to me is because I love to travel.

The urge to travel seems to underlie all of the lifestyle changes I make. I feel almost tangibly drawn to exploring the world. I believe that people who travel extensively gain a whole range of experiences that just don't happen when one stays put. These experiences shape the human mind and lead to a very unique perspective. And I truly believe my Sabarimala trips offer unparalleled life education, providing clarity, better understanding and appreciation of the beauty and wonder of our beautiful world.

On these journeys, I can take a break from my IPhone, IPad and Laptop and literally unplug myself from the irresistible addiction to technology that we all find ourselves so wired into in the modern urban world. On these journeys, I can embark upon new adventures as I experience the treasures of the natural world. Since this journey is not one undertaken on main roads, I often find myself off the well-travelled paths and come upon spontaneous natural discoveries.

The euphoria, excitement and freedom of getting away are priceless. This sense of well-being produces a positive stress, one free of the anxiety caused by work or tensions related to home life. The benefits of travelling have the power of freeing our bodies and minds.

The journey to Sabarimala and back lasts 20 days and, en route, I encounter many other places and cultures around the world. Since I am travelling literally from one end of the world to the other - from North America to Asia - Europe and the Middle East often become exciting stopping points where tasty new food, breathtaking new sights and different sounds help create new experiences and, therefore, new memories. It is true that the photos I take capture the setting in real time but the memories of the exotic smells, sights and sounds stay with me forever.

In addition to the very personal benefits, my trips also provide me with the opportunity to share my experiences with friends and family – here in Canada, in India, the USA, the UAE, Malaysia and beyond. It is indeed a joyful thing to share the experience of a special trip with those we love.

Each year, I also make new friends from around the world. When you travel in the company of like-minded people, those who are as determined, as resilient and as adventurous as you are, they give you the strength and encouragement you need to focus on the strenuous rough terrain through which you are trekking. The Sabarimala trek, though it is open to anyone, cannot, by its very nature, attract those who cannot cope with the difficulties of this journey.

Even though all of us on this journey are on our own, we are never by ourselves. We can always learn from the experts – the gurus or guides who have been on the trek before and are willing to teach and learn along with us. We come home not only with snapshots and souvenirs but also with knowledge and understanding and valuable experiences.

To this day, I look forward to the trek each year with the same fervour, anticipation and exuberance of the innocent 17-year-old that I was when I first made my Sabarimala trek. Each trip allows my imagination to soar since it lets the thrill seeker within me ample time and opportunity for independent exploration.

When we climb Sabarimala, we take in its breathtaking natural beauty, abiding traditions and profoundly hospitable people. We discover the amazing temples dotted throughout the hills. As I explore Sabarimala I am, by default, also able to experience Kerala's Periyar Reserve and its historic and natural treasures while getting 'up close and personal' with the elephants in their natural habitat.

The more I travel, the more I get to learn about the world and its people. Travel expands my awareness, opens me up and prepares me for more diversity. I can never stop exploring and learning about the incredible world in which we live.

The Pilgrimage

The Sabarimala pilgrimage to pay obeisance to Lord Ayyappa symbolizes the journey to heaven and it is one of the most sacred pilgrimage locations in all of India. The Lord Ayyappa Temple is situated on the summit of Mount Sabarimala which is in the midst of 18 hills and surrounded by dense forests.

The origins of the deity Ayyappa can be traced to antiquity. However, it is only in the last five to six decades that the movement has gained momentum and popularity, spreading beyond the parochial limits of the state of Kerala in Southern India.

The Sabarimala shrine is a unique temple in many ways. It is believed to be the place where the Hindu God Ayyappa meditated after killing the powerful demoness, Mahishi. Though this small temple and its surrounding quadrangle take up no more than a few thousand square feet and is situated in inaccessible mountainous forest terrain, it has, since ancient times, brought together many generations of people across India and the world, teaching them about religious harmony, interfaith respect and universal brotherhood.

This temple is, if not the only such place of worship, then definitely a rare example that stands for the strong and lasting camaraderie between three major religions in the state of Kerala in India: Hinduism, Islam and Christianity.

Every year, 50–60 million pilgrims travel to the shrine of Lord Ayyappa on Sabarimala in what has become the second largest pilgrimage phenomenon in the world. The devotees walk barefoot through forests abounding in wildlife and climb precarious paths to reach the temple at the summit.

The absence of any hierarchy, where all are equal before Lord Ayyappa, is striking. Even the deity and the devotee are known by the same name – either Ayyappa or Swamy. This is the only such belief in the entire world. It is in this aspect that Sabarimala becomes more of a reality than a myth.

In today's world, where diverse religious beliefs often lead to war and bloodshed in troubled countries, this is the one temple in the world whose doors are open to all, whatever their beliefs may be. The successful intertwining of rituals in the triumvirate is that of Ayyappa, a Hindu; Vavar, a Muslim and Kochu Thomman, a Christian. This combining of cultures speaks volumes for this simple truth.

Knowing the symbolism of Sabarimala, as I take the journey to the source, helps me understand how each ritual in the journey actually represents the inward spiritual journey to our own source - the consciousness.

The challenges I face in climbing the steep mountains of Sabarimala are similar in many ways to those we all face as we climb our own symbolic mountains in search of our own destiny.

From personal experience I know that the mountainous terrain ahead can seem daunting at times but it is by meeting and overcoming hardships that we confront our strengths and weaknesses, our beliefs and our fundamental values and thereby gain a much better sense of self.

ACE *Insights*   2

Find Your Life Purpose

"Why am I here?"

That is the question all of us ask ourselves. It is just a matter of allowing ourselves the space and time to find out. We are all given different gifts. Our purpose is to figure out what they are and share them with the world.

And when we find our Life Purpose, we have to believe it and live it.

Look at ways to incorporate your passions and talents into your life more regularly. As you do, your Life Purpose will begin to unfold.

1: What do you really enjoy?

Make a list of the things you really like to do. Include what you enjoy about your work, volunteer activities and recreational and artistic pursuits. Include things on the list even if you don't do them now. This list will illuminate for you the things that you love to do or would do simply for the pleasure they bring you.

2: What people do you admire and why do you admire them?

Make a list of as many people as you can think of. Search the list for clues to the common qualities they possess that you appreciate.

You will see that these qualities speak to you because they are a part of your own true path as well and instinctively you know these qualities will take you toward your purpose. Look for and nurture these qualities in yourself. Qualities like the courage to step outside of the box, tell the truth and live out loud will be the action steps that can lead you to your true self and help you attain your passions.

3: What sorts of things do you naturally do without even thinking about them?

Do you have natural talents like an eye for detail, a sense of humor, a nurturing side, the ability to focus intently or a playful personality? Don't be afraid to ask others for their opinions about you. They may see talents in you that you don't see yourself. Once you are aware of your innate talents you can use them in service of your Life Purpose.

4: Do you make a conscious effort to pursue your passions?

Once you have taken the time to compile your lists, spend 10 minutes each morning doing something from one of the lists. Draw, sing, dance, tell the truth about something you've been concealing or thank someone you've been appreciating silently. Perhaps even take that risk and call the girl or guy you want to get to know better.

5: Do you pay attention to what you feel?

If you're living your Life Purpose, you'll feel exhilarated, excited, happy and alive. If you're not feeling these things, examine your life more closely and see if perhaps there are things you have been avoiding looking at because they're too scary. Often, a professional can help us sort out the difficult things that are keeping us from living a fulfilling life.

6: Are you afraid to take that next step?

It's normal to feel scared when stepping into your Life Purpose. If it's worth doing, you're probably going to feel apprehensive about doing it. If you can convert that apprehension into the energy you need to take the next step, you are half way there.

Action cures fear. Facing your fears makes you powerful. When we acknowledge our strengths and weaknesses, we can embrace our strengths and work to strengthen our weaknesses.

Identifying your Life Purpose

When you are doing the things you are good at and that come naturally to you, you feel energized and rejuvenated.

When you go one step further and use your unique skills and talents to help others to further their dreams, it is then that you are living your Life Purpose.

How do you know what your Life Purpose is?
Ask yourself these questions.

- If you could do one thing for the rest of your life, what would it be?
- When you have spare time, what do you want to do?
- What are you willing to do over and over again until you perfect it?
- What subject do you enjoy talking about and could talk about for hours?
- At the end of your life, what would be the one thing you would be most happy about having done or having been?
- Who do you most want to help, enable or reach?
- What five life experiences have given you the greatest sense of fulfillment or growth?

For me, spirituality was the key in finding my Life Purpose, my unique way of serving my fellow man.

There are things that we cannot control and there are things that each of us are not very good at. In difficult life situations, it is comforting to know that the only thing that can get us through is the knowledge that there is a higher power and we are an important part of that plan.

So far, every difficult situation that has arisen in my life has led me to something better that I was not even expecting.

The first year I climbed Sabarimala, I felt overwhelmed. Today, I look forward to it. Mountain climbing has become the very real metaphor for my spiritual journey. Every step in the hike leads me nearer the mountain peak as all knowledge in my quest leads me to a higher level of understanding. I can continue to climb because of the strength of my spiritual beliefs. They help me find the answers to why something is happening and help me believe that I do not always have to be in control.

A Whole Universe of Possibilities.

*"Twenty years from now you will be more disappointed
by the things that you didn't do than by the ones you did do."*

Mark Twain

Another way to understand yourself better and learn new ways of looking at your life is through travel.

Travel opens your mind and strengthens your body and your soul.

From the beginning of human endeavour, people have followed their urges to see the world, to understand their surroundings and to be part of their environment. New worlds, different civilizations and cultures were there for those who kept an open mind and had the courage to look for them. Their reasons for travel were vastly different and yet remain the same: to explore and conquer the unknown.

Especially in the fast-paced urban lifestyle in which most of us find ourselves today, travel is important. It can greatly improve our physical health and rejuvenate our bodies. Perhaps even more importantly, it can do wonders for our mental health and our well being. Importantly, it is also a major healer when it comes to achieving clarity, inner peace and re-gaining a stable state of mind.

Some Benefits of Travel

1. The great escape

Travel is the perfect escape from everyday life. It doesn't matter if it is only two hours away or two days away. Any escape from what we are used to can greatly improve our lives and mental well-being on so many levels. It allows us time and distance to rejuvenate our souls and clear our minds from the stress of everyday routine.

2. The great outdoors

Travel is also a great source of movement and exercise. At home, we fall into the doom and gloom of rainy days or cold winters and we just don't feel like exercising. But when we are travelling, the possiilities are greater that you will be on your feet, walking and exploring. Travelling gets the blood flowing because it requires us to be active. We are more likely to be outdoors and motivated to be moving around new environments than when we are at home or trapped by our work.

Exercise is known to increase happy feelings and boost adrenaline, a hormone with many health benefits including the ability to cause a feeling of well-being. Therefore, a trip away will greatly improve your mood. The world is our playground and the more we venture out into it, the happier we feel.

3. Personal growth

Travelling affords us the opportunity to see new places, experience new cultures and open our minds and hearts to the amazing beauty our world provides. When we change our rhythm of life, which we do when we travel, we can find the time to reflect, to make peace with the past and also to learn new life skills. Time away is very important for personal growth.

4. Meeting the world

Man is a social animal. We are not meant to be alone.

Isolation can lead to many health problems including depression. When we travel, we are opening ourselves up to the world and it brings us numerous opportunities to meet new people and expand our network.

More significantly, travel can teach us how to communicate with others, even if they don't speak the same language, eat the same foods or worship the same deities. It can help us be courageous in the face of the unknown when we realize that, even when there are differences between people, we are all the same underneath.

It can be daunting to talk to a stranger but, if you don't know where to find food or the way back to your base, you have to approach people. This can lead to social bravery. Being in a foreign land forces us to adapt and talk to strangers.

5. Learning to judge

Astute travellers have to quickly learn how to trust some people and how to stay away from others. It is a life skill that atrophies when one does not venture out of one's comfort zone.

When you travel, you not only pick up local customs, you have to pay attention to the body language and nuances of other people's behavior. You have to learn to trust your own hunches when you are in an unfamiliar place.

At home, you generally have others to lean on. You can trust the familiar and already know the places to go for the best food, the best and safest route to take. When travelling, you have to actively seek out the things you want. There's no other option. You have to rely on yourself, trust yourself and your abilities. Honing these qualities translates nicely into making effective decisions during emergencies or hard times.

6. Learning to rely on others

Even though the idea of relying on others seems to conflict with the idea of self-reliance, really it is just the end result of the confidence you acquire from relying on yourself and trusting your instincts.

Once you overcome your fear of talking to strangers, you can put your life skills to work by learning to communicate with others and judging whose advice is sound. When you ask everyone you meet for their recommendation on the best route, you become the recipient of the collective knowledge of 10 locals. That's better than most guidebooks!

Travel and the skills it teaches you make you a person who can talk easily with strangers, can rely on their instincts to make sound judgments and has the confidence to handle almost any situation quickly and effectively.

MILESTONE

3

The Research

"Awaken your own mind, amass your own experience, and decide for yourself your own path."

The Atharva Veda

In 1987, when I decided to take my first trip, I prepared myself by acquiring as much knowledge as I could about the Sabarimala Trek. And so began my research. Today, as I prepare for my 27th trip, I am still researching and still learning. Here is what I have learned so far.

Sabarimala

Sabarimala (Mount Sabari) is 3,000 feet above sea level and lies in the Sahyadris, the Western Ghats, in the state of Kerala in Pathanamthitta District.

The origins and significance of the various customs practiced by the pilgrims to Sabarimala are based on five belief systems: the Shaivites, the Shaktists, the Vaishnavites, the Buddhists and the Jainists. All five systems merge in the rituals observed by the pilgrims to Sabarimala.

Shaivites - The chains the pilgrims wear around their necks comes from the *Rudraksha* chain worn by the Shaivites.

Shaktists - The offerings to Kaduthaswamy is taken from the beliefs of the Shaktists, the devotees of Shakti.

Vaishnavites - The strict fasting, penance and self-restraint is taken from the beliefs of the Vaishnavites.

Buddhists - Another name of Lord Ayyappa is Sastha which means Buddha. This speaks to the reach of Buddhist beliefs to this part of the world. The constant and repeated utterance of prayers is prevalent among the Buddhists.

Jainists - *Ahimsa* is taken from the Jainists.

The rituals

Those who decide to climb Sabarimala need to observe strict penance, fasting, self-restraint and celibacy for a minimum period of 41 days between the holy *Margazhi* months of November through January.

Through the observation of these strict adherences, one learns to control one's senses by giving up human desires. He remolds himself. Once he reaches his

Ahimsa: The principle of nonviolence toward all living things.

destination, he realizes **Thatwamasi** The meaning of *Thathwamasi* – 'That is You'.

It is the concept of Supreme consciousness. A self-realized person has all his thoughts under control. He recognizes his divinity as inscribed in the Sabarimala Temple. Thus he recognizes the enormous power, restraint and resilience from within.

Namasthe: Derived from the Sanskrit language, the literal meaning of the word is, 'I bow to you'. It can be broken up into two Sanskrit words – Namas, meaning to bow and Te, meaning to you.

Thus, its real connotation is: 'I bow to you out of respect'.

The popular Hindu greeting performed all over India and by Indians all over the world. It is done by pressing two hands together and holding them near the heart. The act communicates to the world: "You and I are One. I salute and worship the God within you which is a mirror image of myself".

It is customary for all pilgrims to Sabarimala to greet each other with a *Namasthe*.

Namasthe is both a formal and an informal greeting all over India. You can say this to anyone irrespective of age. Normally when you say *Namaste* to anybody, you press both your palms together with all the fingers pointing upwards in front of your chest, bow your head slightly, looking at the person you are saying *Namaste* to. Even if you simply perform the *Namaste* gesture with your hands, without actually saying the word, it will mean the same thing.

Though saying *Namaste* to others in our daily lives is a part of the Indian protocol, many believe it also has religious and spiritual connotations. According to this school of thought, when you greet someone with *Namaste*, you actually seek to recognize a common divinity within the other person. You are saying: 'You and I are One. I salute and worship the God within you which is a mirror image of myself.'

During the actual trek, the entire journey is undertaken without any exuberance. This reveals the patience, endurance and mental strength a man can achieve.

Each devotee carries on his head a sacred *Irumudi* - a cloth bag containing *Pooja,* symbolic items such as coconuts, dried fruit, sandalwood paste and turmeric. The coconuts filled with ghee, or clarified butter, which one has carried in the *Irumudi* during the climb are thrown into the blazing hearth at the summit. This act symbolizes the burning off of one's selfishness.

A bath in the Pamba River at the end of the pilgrimage symbolizes driving away the sins one has committed in one's life.

Preparing for the Climb

Certainly, climbing Sabarimala is an extraordinary physical, mental and emotional test. Climbers must cope with constant stress, sleep deprivation, extreme weather, fatigue, wild animals and various other obstacles for over a four-day period.

Success on Sabarimala is very much about having the proper mindset and focus. It is essential that climbers develop strong mental skills and apply them before and while climbing the mountain. Being physically strong and logistically prepared are also critical aspects of mounting a successful summit.

In fact, a successful Sabarimala sojourn depends on 10 critical components, four of which are part of the preparation before the climb and six that are crucial during the assent in order to reach the Pinnacle of Excellence.

The Preparation

1. Visualizing, Verbalizing and Virtualizing

Part of the strategy of planning for the climb is visualizing the ascent with a razor-sharp focus. Seeing and feeling oneself execute the climb through repeated chants and visualizations is a common practice in mental preparation prior to the actual climb.

All successful climbers use the imagined experience of the climb as a means to helping them perform well during the difficult phases of the Sabarimala trek.

2. Detailed planning

Part of what makes a successful Sabarimala climber, or climber of any mountain for that matter, is the ability to stay focused, remain confident and be thoroughly prepared. By making sure your preparations are complete and that you have researched and learned all you can about what lies ahead, you can be confident that you know what it is you are trying to do, have a clear picture of what your plan is and can prepare for all the possible things that can go wrong.

3. Mental fortitude

Developing mental toughness is the most important skill one can cultivate in preparation for climbing Sabarimala.

One must understand the importance of developing mental strength and the skills that are required for focus during adversity. This fortitude is important to success in many pursuits but it is an essential preparation strategy in successful high altitude climbing. The consequences of error, of losing focus even temporarily, can result in serious mishap.

4. Hard physical training

Climbers must continually strive to stretch their physical limits and be able to increase their ability to withstand discomfort. By pushing themselves physically, they gain emotional strength as well.

It is no secret that such arduous climbing involves a great deal of pain and discomfort. To undertake such a trek, you have to be able to endure it. And this skill is unique to climbing a mountain because in no other sport is there so much discomfort and potential for tragedy. From the physical endurance required to climb almost 24 hours straight, through the day and night, the constant changing and unpredictable weather, the extreme periods of fatigue and chance encounters with wild animals during the summit push, you have to be strong psychologically, mentally and physically.

Each year, between November and January, I train by pushing myself harder and harder to reach these goals. On days when I reach the point where I have had enough and want to back off, I consciously push myself through that threshold.

Over the past 26 years, pushing that threshold has had a positive effect on the way I climb the hills. So much so that, sometimes, experiencing hardship can be a reward in itself. Experiencing and embracing the pain makes me feel alive. And, when I feel alive and vibrant, I can push forward.

The Ascent

1. Emotional toughness

On the actual ascent, climbers must be able to rely on their mental, physical and emotional strength to overcome the setbacks when they come face to face with obstacles that can impede their success or actually cause them physical harm. Developing their mental toughness helps them prepare for the challenges of the arduous climb.

Having positive experiences where they have been able to get through adversity gives them the confidence to say, "Yes, I can do it." Accepting and thriving through the pain has helped me numerous times endure the challenges I face on the mountain.

2. Focus

While on the climb, focus is an essential skill. Climbers must learn to get into a zone, breathe properly, monitor their pace, direct their physical and mental energy to the immediate challenge in front of them and concentrate their attention to the task at hand.

Focus, therefore, is a step-by-step process which allows the climber to eliminate distractions, stay with the task at hand and achieve their objectives one by one, day by day, moment by moment.

In honing my focus, I visualize climbing Sabarimala one step at a time. I definitely want to be focused on summiting, but I understand that I really need to focus on the day to day and that this is the key to being successful.

3. Short-term goals

It is extremely important to set short-term goals while climbing the mountain and these specific, relevant, daily goals change through the entire expedition to the summit. All climbers agree that setting short-term goals are crucial to the success on the mountain as this ongoing process enables us to remain focused on the task at hand and not become overwhelmed by the size of the ultimate goal or the immensity of the experience.

4. Learning from past experience

On every climb, we learn more about what works and what doesn't. Through their numerous previous experiences in high altitude environments, climbers gain a strong foundation of knowledge. I draw upon this wealth of experience whenever I am faced with challenging situations.

It is also important to draw on the past experiences of other climbers. It does not take long, for example, to learn that you have to drink a lot of water on the climb. When you don't drink, you become dehydrated and that affects your stride and your ability to acclimatize. As a novice, I found that the accumulation of experience and the lessons gained from others proved a valuable asset and investment in climbing Sabarimala.

5. Belief in your capacity

When you undertake such a momentous mission, it is important to believe in yourself and your capacity to complete your goal. This is a key factor in the success on the mountain. When the obstacles come, I have to decide how much I believe in my dream. All the preparation, physical and mental, that has gone into the process gives me confidence on the mountain when distress and pain could be a hindrance.

On the actual ascent, there is good level of discomfort due to the altitude and this hampered my first few ascents. I was unsettled and stressed by the discomfort. Now, after the first few kilometres, I am able to work on my acclimatization and my response to pain. After so many climbs, I think I have it down to a science. I have learned to absorb pain by slowing down, drinking more and altering my sleeping arrangements.

But there are always new things to learn. The biggest challenge remains discerning harmless pain from warning bells of something more serious. What is danger pain and what is just discomfort? Experience leads to more confidence in my ability to judge.

In fact, the strategy of living and thriving at high altitude is now part of the appeal of climbing Sabarimala. I now know that, in high altitude climbing, discomfort is a normal part of the experience and I accept the discomfort as part of the process. Experience breeds confidence.

6. Team support

Working together with and supporting teammates on the mountain is an important component of reaching the summit. All the climbers who walk with me have overcome obstacles on the path to the summit with the encouragement and strength of their teammates. For these climbers, supporting one another and believing in one another as climbers is an important element of their success on the mountain.

Even on the tough, two-hour descent, climbers know that their journey is not over until all the climbers have returned from the summit of the mountain to base camp. They also know that support is not always about being nice to one another; it is about challenging one another and motivating one another.

ACE *Insights* **3**

Learning Important Life Lessons

Accepting what is

There is only so much we can affect. What we cannot change or influence, we must learn to accept. Taking this road will lead us towards peace.

It is only when we start accepting those things that we cannot alter that we begin to feel relief from the stress and anxiety brought on by trying to change the unchangeable. There are things we can do to help with the process of finding peace.

1. Meditation

Meditating is a very important activity that can change your life. Twenty minutes daily of this amazing activity can have an enormous impact on all areas of your life.

Living in the modern world with the pressures of work and family life can often leave us with many worries and dilemmas that occupy our minds more than is healthy or wise. By practicing meditation, we can learn to manage these forces impacting our thoughts and emotions.

Simply turn everything off, sit back, close your eyes and clear your mind of every single thought. Although this is not always easy to do, if you practice focusing on the emptiness, you will be surprised what a mere 20 minutes of meditation can do to turn things around for you. Professional guided meditation CDs are also helpful in leading you through the meditation process so that you can reach a level of peacefulness.

2. Spending time in nature

Most of us spend so much time confined in buildings of steel and concrete and brick that we often forget where we come from and where you feel most at home. It is natural for us to be in nature. That is why it feels so good and why it feels so peaceful when you take a walk in a park or bike on a trail in the forest. Even just taking the time to look at the natural world around us in the city can bring us serenity.

From the window of my home office, I see a sturdy tree. Watching its stillness, with the breeze calmly blowing through its branches, is a sight that not only inspires me but one that calms me within.

If you feel overwhelmed, being in nature where there is an abundance of trees and listening to the sounds and sights of the natural world, even if it is just a large park in the city, can afford you peace.

3. Taming the ego

Peak Point

Mountains remind us that there is always something or someone bigger than we are.

The ego is like a horse. If you can learn to tame it, then you will be able to ride it easily and it will take you where you need to go. If you let it run wild – it will take off like a rocket and perhaps claim you as a victim. Control the ego and you can become the master of your own destiny.

No matter how successful you become, staying humble opens you up to future growth and opportunity. But keeping the ego in check takes work. Here are some of the steps I practice to tame the wild ego inside.

Practice generosity – Give of your time, energy and resources. Do good deeds quietly for others, not for reward but without expectation of praise or recognition.

Practice unconditional love – Try to be more conscious of how you love those people important in your life. When you are able to love someone apart from what the benefits may be for you or despite the flaws you see in them, the ego is transcended.

Practice compassion and kindness – Be aware and ready to help others in need and recognize how you can be of service. Kindness is its own reward. It doesn't matter who they are, people close to us or complete strangers, but any act of kindness and good will eases our way towards peace. A simple smile can make a difference, not only to the recipient but to us as well.

Practice seeing yourself as part of a higher power – Self-transcendence is a major facet of overcoming the ego. Aligning yourself with an authentic spiritual belief allows for a shift from a focus on the self to a focus on others.

Both Buddhism and Hinduism share the belief that, in order to reach enlightenment or Nirvana, we must transcend the ego. No matter how we define ego, one thing is certain. According to these beliefs, until we tame the ego, we will not find inner peace or a happier existence.

4. Think outwardly

When we have a really bad day or feel emotionally overwhelmed, it is often helpful to remind ourselves that we have a great deal to be grateful for. When we are consumed by our problems, we cannot see beyond ourselves. But when we look outwards, that helps to remind us how big the world really is and that we are just a tiny part of the whole picture.

Although we often feel that, if we could only solve our own problems, we could be happy but, truly, we can never find peace by being self-consumed and only worrying about our own needs and wants. When we begin to genuinely care about other people, the goodness we all carry inside comes to the surface. This only helps to solidify our inner peace.

On my Sabarimala trips, I find innumerable occasions to help someone, whether it is offering money to some destitute person or buying food for someone. In return, my offerings make it possible for me to also accept acts of charity from others.

When we are deeply involved with ourselves, we are blind to the needs of others.

When we help other people, we stop focusing on ourselves and realize that our life isn't so bad after all. There is great peace and wisdom in thinking of and caring about other people.

5. Stay hopeful

Hope is something you can never afford to lose. Many times, I feel like giving up while I am climbing and it is only hope that keeps me going.

Peak Point

Hope is always better than hopelessness.

With hope you always have a path forward. Whenever we are overwhelmed by stress and the pressure of life, we forget that hope always exists and that we may find the solution for today's problem more easily tomorrow.

When we have hope, we can see that terrible times are only temporary and that things can improve. This knowledge lifts us from negativity and brings us immense peace.

6. Keep learning

One thing that provides us with much stress in life is the fact that we always worry about not having all the answers. We feel particularly powerless when we make mistakes and blame ourselves for not having known the right thing to do.

Just accepting that we do not know everything and that failure can often be the best way to learn can be a tremendous step towards avoiding panic and achieving inner peace.

We must be aware that we can grow as a person each and every day. Leaving ourselves open to that possibility can also provide us with a great sense of power. Accepting that life is one big journey of never-ending opportunities for learning brings us closer to experiencing true serenity.

7. Live in the present moment

Peak Point

If we are not green, we rot.

Most of the time, what we worry about is related to something that has happened in the past or something that may happen in the future. Being able to live in the present moment alleviates those worries. If we tell ourselves that we cannot change things from the past, we may learn to accept them. If we understand that it is pointless to worry about something that we are not even sure will ever happen, we will be better able to focus on the problems that need solving today.

There are always valleys and peaks in life. That's the nature of existence. But if we take our lives one day at a time then we can learn to pace ourselves to deal with one thing at a time.

MILESTONE

4

The Mentorship

"Matru Devo Bhava, Pitru Devo Bhava, Acharya Devo Bhava"
["After the mother and the father, revere your coach like God"]

Sanskrit verse from the Upanishads,
Hindu scriptures, 5000 BC

The Guruswamy

In very simple words, a Guru is revered as a teacher, coach, mentor and much more.

The word *Guru* is derived from the Sanskrit language and has a deep spiritual meaning. *Gu* denotes the spiritual ignorance of most of humankind. *Ru* represents the radiance of spiritual knowledge that dispels the spiritual ignorance.

The Guru is the One who dispels the darkness of ignorance in humanity and bestows upon it life-inspiring experiences and knowledge.

In ancient India, the Guru was a spiritually evolved guide. Along with the knowledge of various subjects, he also taught his students how to live a disciplined and principled life. A Guru was the spiritual guiding force in the life of his students.

The Guruswamy takes one to the Lord; he leads his student towards the divinity.

As the Hindu Dharma tells us, the role of the Guru in the life of his students is much more than just teacher.

A teacher takes responsibility for your growth
A Guru makes you responsible for your own growth

A teacher gives you things you do not have and require
A Guru takes away things you have and do not require

A teacher answers your questions
A Guru questions your answers

A teacher helps you get out of the maze
A Guru destroys your maze

A teacher requires obedience and discipline from the pupil
A Guru requires trust and humility from the pupil

A teacher clothes you and prepares you for the outer journey
A Guru strips you naked and prepares you for the inner journey

A teacher is a guide on the path
A Guru is the pointer to the way

A teacher sends you on the road to success
A Guru sends you on the road to freedom

A teacher explains the world and its nature to you
A Guru explains yourself and your nature to you

When the course is over, you are thankful to the teacher
When the course is over, you are grateful to the Guru

A teacher makes you understand how to move about in the world
A Guru shows you where you stand in relation to the world

A teacher instructs you
A Guru constructs you

A teacher sharpens your mind
A Guru opens your mind

A teacher shows you the way to prosperity
A Guru shows the way to serenity

A teacher reaches your mind
A Guru touches your soul

A teacher gives you knowledge
A Guru makes you wise

A teacher gives you maturity
A Guru returns you to innocence

A teacher instructs you on how to solve problems
A Guru shows you how to resolve issues

A teacher is a systematic thinker
A Guru is a lateral thinker

One can always find a teacher
A Guru has to find and accept you

A teacher leads you by the hand
A Guru leads you by example

Guruswamy Vaakyam Pramaanam:
The Guruswamy's words are final.

Shishyas: Disciples.

Shlokas: Hymns.

Pooja: Prayers.

Maala: Holy Beads.

Yatra: Pilgrimage.

In the Hindu tradition, the concept of Guru Dakshina is very ancient and unique to the Indian culture. Guru Dakshina is meant to serve as a way of repaying, showing respect and giving thanks to the Guru.

For Swamis, giving Guru Dakshina to the Guru forms a very important part of the culture.

In order to show gratitude towards the Guru, we need to offer Guru Dakshina more than once.

In total, it is a practice that a Sishya [Devotee] has to pay respects to his Guruswamy and pay him Guru Dakshina 8 times during the SabarimalaYatra, the trek.

When a teacher finishes with you, you graduate. When a Guru finishes with you, you celebrate.

In the Sabarimala pilgrimage, the Guruswamy – the mentor – is the supreme of all and pilgrims strictly follow their Guruswamy's instructions from the first days of their fasting until they reach home again.

The whole concept of Sabarimala revolves around the Guruswamy who has a significant role to play in the Ayyappa legend. It is only after receiving the blessings of a Guruswamy that one can wear the Maala, the Holy beads. Without him, the pilgrimage cannot be completed.

The Guruswamy is usually a senior person who has undertaken the pilgrimage to Sabarimala no less than seven consecutive years using the traditional long route. It is important that pilgrims gain knowledge from him in all the aspects of the

Pilgrimage. One should serve and edify the *Guruswamy* physically, mentally and verbally.

Pilgrims are expected to give the *Guruswamy* the due respect and reverence that he deserves. All his instructions should be carried out without fail. He enlightens the *Shishyas*, about the austerities to be followed, teaches them the *Shlokas* and how to perform the *Pooja*, He prepares them for the pilgrimage mentally and physically and leads the pilgrims safely and comfortably to Sabarimala.

Guruswamy and Guru Dakshina

Guru Dakshina is a revered Hindu tradition of acknowledgment, respect and thanks between a student and his Guru. This reciprocity and exchange between student and teacher is not exclusively monetary and may include other forms of thanks as well.

The *Guru Dakshina* is given for the first time when the Guru formally accepts the pilgrim for the Sabarimala *yatra*, the pilgrimage. It is also given at various other significant times during the *Yatra*.

While wearing the *Maala*

- While taking the *Irumudi* - Kettu Nerai
- At Erumeli at the start of Yatra after the *Darshanam*
- At Azhudha river
- At Pampa after the *Snanam* and while starting the journey
- At Sannidhanam after the *Abhishekam*
- While removing the *Maala*

It is the duty of every Ayyappa *bhaktha* to follow all these rules strictly and earn the grace of the Guruswamy. I continue to offer *Guru Dakshina* to my various *Guruswamys* at various stages before, during and after my *Yatra* each year.

ACE *Insights*   *4*

Wisdom passed through the generations by various Guruswamys

Over the years, I have had the good fortune of trekking with many Guruswamys and I have learned something priceless from each one of them.

Lessons learned while climbing the mountain can teach you about life too. Let me share with you some lessons I have learned while climbing my mountains, both real and symbolic.

Insight: Expect to experience setbacks and learn to turn them into stepping stones

We only conquer even the greatest obstacle one step at a time. You don't climb well by looking to the summit. It's too overwhelming. You focus on the next leg of the route.

We have boundless resources with which to face life. Each time I experience fatigue and an inner voice tells me to turn back or hire a cab to cover the rest of the distance, I pause, take a break and move forward. At times like these I know I need to remind myself about the power that has been placed within us.

Insight: Remember why you do it and use that to fuel your journey

I always try to take time, especially when the going is tough, to just stop and soak in the beauty and grandeur of what nature has made.

One of the most important things we can do in life is figure out what it is we want to do more than anything else and then work to accomplish it.

We can only do this when we know, not only how to do what we do well, but also why we are doing it. Knowing our goal will also serve to focus us and help us make good choices along the way.

Our goal should be something that we find satisfying and fulfilling and brings us joy. And when we identify it, we should write it down and read it over every so often. That way we can think about it, especially at those times when we run up against our own personal mountains.

Finally, develop a strong trust in your instincts and insights.

Insight: Appreciate that people share a common humanity

I have had the opportunity to travel many times and learn from many people on those travels. We have travelled together under the best of conditions and under the worst and most extreme conditions.

Develop the courage to challenge both yourself and those around you. Even though you want to be persistent when pursuing your lofty goal, you must also have the flexibility to see things in new ways.

In this experience lies my abiding belief in the goodness and greatness of the human spirit. We live in a world where people often live separate lives, in separate cultures, but we are bound together in a common humanity.

Success and happiness in life will come only when you find a purpose that extends beyond yourself.

Insight: Crisis can be opportunity

We have so much to gain if we recognize that we can learn from our differences.

In the Chinese language, one of the oldest written languages on earth, the word for crisis is *weiji*. This word actually consists of two characters: *wei,* which means danger and *ji*, which means opportunity.

In one word, both warning and hope is expressed. Certainly with every crisis, whether personal, national or international, comes danger. But with every crisis also comes the opportunity to make things better.

Peak Point

We can sink to the depths of our resistance or rise to the heights of our challenge.

Mountains remind us that there is always something bigger to conquer. Our problem might seem huge but we must always be aware that someone else might have a worse problem than ours.

If we manage to overcome our struggle, we can find encouragement to tackle the next one. In fact, we can often find help ourselves by serving someone else in their need.

Mountains won't take your challenges away but they'll teach you a lot about facing and overcoming them.

MILESTONE

The Journey Begins - *The First Steps*

"The sharp edge of a razor is difficult to pass over;
thus the wise say, the path to Salvation is hard."

Katha-Upanishad,
Hindu Scriptures, 5000 BC

I believe the reason the Sabarimala Temple attracts millions of devotees each year is that it has an inexplicable mystique, is not easily accessible and has an enduring aura of propagating universal brotherhood among all of God's creations. This pilgrimage becomes like a yearly addiction. Even though at the end of the exhausting trek you may declare that there will be no *Maala* for you next year, even you don't believe it!

The Sabarimala shrine has continued to teach generations of people across India and the world about religious harmony, inter faith respect and universal brotherhood. This temple is, if not the only, definitely a rare example that stands for the strong and lasting camaraderie between three major religions in the state of Kerala in India – Hinduism, Islam and Christianity.

As soon as I started my research, I began to understand the depth and distinctiveness of the Sabarimala Pilgrimage which demands a combination of prolonged penance and systemic practice of its pilgrims which is observed under strict rules.

Maala or Rudraksha Maala :
The necklace made of holy
beads. Darshanam: The holy
sighting, the viewing.

Sannidhanam: The summit
of Sabarimala, the sanctum
sanctorum of Sabarimala.

Every tradition and practice associated with Sabarimala has profound meaning, based on the Vedanta philosophical traditions concerned with realization, as well as pragmatic ideals, meanings and implications. The system prescribes the details of how to carry the offerings to the Swamy, the precise food articles and the other essential items allowed on the trek, the journey itself across five tough, inhospitable mountains, the rituals undertaken on the way, the offerings made along the route and everything else that is related to this spiritual journey.

Then the trek itself is undertaken along challenging terrain through steep hills in the dense forest and can only be accomplished through strict commitment and

Murali Murthy

focus in order to attain the *Sannidhanam* experience. The pilgrimage culminates at the *Darshanam* of the deity.

These two disciplines of penance and trekking are combined with the aim of giving renewal and rejuvenation to one's mind and body. Trekking along the difficult terrain of the mountain is an essential ingredient of the process where the purposeful lack of facilities and the difficult climb contribute to the devotee's spiritual strengthening and awakening.

A true Ayyappa devotee is fully aware of all the natural difficulties en route to Sabarimala and even those on their first trek understand that they are following a unique system that guides this extraordinary pilgrimage and they have respect and reverence for the experienced guides who lead them on this journey.

No true devotee of Ayyappa wants to dilute any of the difficulties of the pilgrimage he faces along the way. One never thinks of the comforts that are lacking during this holy trek and realizes that the ordeals he encounters only helps him in his communion with the Swamy and with cleansing his character and attitude in preparation for the final goal: to achieve peace at the end.

The first steps

The pilgrimage begins even before one takes the first physical step towards the temple with the *Virutham*, the 41-day fast of penance in advance of the pilgrimage. This penance encompasses a strict regimen that includes mental, physical and spiritual preparations and must be followed thoroughly during this period.

Bhaktha: Devotee.

Virutham: The fasting process.

Virutha Kaalam / Mandala Kaalam: the 41-day fasting period.

Some say the pilgrimage to Sabarimala is over before it begins, meaning its blessings are sown during the elaborate preparation for it with the intense *Mandala Kaalam* which lasts 41 days and beyond and can test the patience and character of many. That is why the pilgrimage is more like a celebration for completing the preparation for the trek, the rigours of *Mandala Kaalam*.

As I start preparing for my pilgrimage, I begin learning about the significance behind each activity.

The pilgrimage regulations

First, every pilgrim has to take certain vows and seek the permission and the blessings of his elders or his Guruswamy. The vow, taken at least 45 days before ascending the Holy 18 Steps to the *Sannidhanam*, carries some mandatory rules about the austerities and regulations which the pilgrim must observe before the pilgrimage begins so he can become pure and strong in both the physical and mental sphere.

Then, with every new day, with every preparation, comes a new list of do's and don'ts.

1. The devotee must cap all carnal desires and strictly follow celibacy. He must frequently chant the mantra, *"Swamiye Saranam Ayyappa"*.

2. During the *Deeksha*, the devotee must wear black or saffron clothes, wear the *Rudraksha maala* around his neck. Once he wears it, the vows must be observed completely.

It is said that a devotee on this pilgrimage is as old as the number of times he has made the trip to the holy mountain. The minute you wear the *Rudraksha maala*, you become a Sage, a Swamy, an Ayyappa. You are untouched by evil thoughts and evil spirits. You become one with the divine and you behave responsibly, irrespective of your age.

3. Austerity and abstinence - the devotee must eat only *Saathwick* and abstain from meat, alcohol and tobacco and intoxicants and physical or verbal violence in any form. Food becomes only a means to live. The devotee must keep food to a minimum and only for the sake of health, not for variety and taste. Not only non-vegetarian food is prohibited but food should be *Saathwick* – basic and pure with no condiments and enhancers (i.e., no onion, garlic etc.).

4. On the first day of *Virutham*, the Fasting Period, the devotee must rise early, bathe, pray to the family deity and perform a *Pooja* to the holy *Maala*. He will be accompanied to the temple by his Guruswamy and receive his *Maala* from him. Wearing the *Maala* denotes that the devotee becomes Lord Ayyappa and must thus lead a pious life.

Those devotees who are desirous of worshipping Lord Ayyappa on *Makara Vilakku* day may continue their *Virutham* until that day. Without a proper *Virutham*, it is a sacrilege to visit the temple or climb the Holy 18 Steps.

Deeksha: Holy Period.

Saathwick: Vegan food in its prisitne form.

Maala Dharanam: Wearing the beads.

5. The devotee is obligated to treat all co-devotees as Lord Ayyappa with respect and serve them in every way. Calling everyone *Ayyappa* or *Swami* should come from the heart and cannot be just a mere ritualistic address. He must be humble despite the respect and privileges accorded to him as a Sabarimala pilgrim.

All our activities should be Ayyappa-centric during the time of fasting. Throughout the 41 days required to complete the *Mandala Vrutham*, contemplation of Lord Ayyappa should be the only focus of a devotee.

6. *Maala Dharanam* is performed generally on the first auspicious day according to the date of the *Yatra*. Maala Dharanam is generally done at one's home or the Guruswamy's home during a *Pooja* or at a common place of worship like a temple.

No spiritual practice is successful without the blessings of a Guru. So, after blessings of Guru, one has to wear the Maala through 'His Own' Guruswamy.

My first few days

Each year, I put on the Holy *Maala* on the 14th of November.

Then, for 41 days, or more, I prepare for a serene spiritual existence by making the appropriate adjustments to my life routines.

I begin my preparations by bathing twice daily, once in the morning and once in the evening, doing at least a simple *Pooja* and calling out *Saranams*.

> *Irumudi: The cloth bag worn on the head.*
>
> *Irumudi Kettu Nerai: The process of wearing the Irumudi.*
>
> *Makara Vilakku: January 14.*
>
> *Yatra: 41 days before the date of Darshan, the holy sighting.*
>
> *Saranams: Holy chants.*

I visit the temple regularly and abstain from indulgences. I never smoke or drink alcohol (except on rare social occasions) so that is not particularly difficult but I am used to eating non-vegetarian food. Now I must subdue all my cravings.

Prior to leaving home for Sabarimala, my *Irumudi* is filled at the temple or in my own *Pooja* room. The ceremony is conducted with the assistance of the Guruswamy amidst chanting of *'Swamiye Saranam Ayyappa'.*

Irumudi Kettu Nerai

The *Irumudi Kettu Nerai* is a cloth bag that is worn on the head by each pilgrim. It contains items such as coconuts, ghee, dry fruit, sandalwood paste and turmeric for making offerings and meagre provisions for the pilgrim. It is a unique process of the Sabarimala journey. One has to be very precise and devoted in this aspect. The Holy 18 Steps cannot be climbed if you are not carrying an *Irumudi Kettu*. Only a Guru designate can fill the rice in the Kettu Nerai. The *Nei* (*Ghee*) should be filled only by the devotee and no one else.

The *Irumudi* is carried on the head with due reverence. It is the very form of Ayyappa and we are all trained to give utmost respect to the *Irumudi*. All the results of our *Virutham* are instilled in the coconut and the ghee that we carry. The custom of carrying ghee in the coconut is an age-old and unique tradition.

Irumudi Kettu is divided into two parts. The front pouch and the rear pouch.

The front pouch is marked with the symbol `OM' for identification. It is meant for stocking *Pooja* articles such as coconuts filled with *ghee*, camphor, raw rice, *kadali*, *aval*, *pori*, sandal paste, incense sticks, *vibhuti*, *kumkum*, turmeric powder, jaggery, *kalkkandom* and coins for *Dakshina*.

During the *Mandala Kaalam,* the Guruswamy prepares an offering of ghee in a very special way. He husks and cleans a coconut and pours the milk out through a small pierced hole. He then fills the coconut with ghee and seals it shut with wax. Throughout the pilgrimage, the devotee carries one, two or three of these ghee-filled coconuts and pours it on the Lord's idol at Sabarimala. The coconut represents the human body and the ghee represents the *Aatma*.

Nei (Ghee): Clarified cow's butter.

Kadali: Plantain.

Aval: Flattened rice.

Pori: Rice flakes.

Vibhuti: Sacred ash.

Kumkum: Vermillion.

Kalkkandom: Candied sugar.

Aatma: Soul.

The ghee-filled coconut symbolizes man's ego shrouding his soul essence. When the ghee is released from the coconut and anoints the icon of Lord Ayyappa, the essence of the soul of the devotee is said to unite with the essence of God, thus bringing the pilgrimage to its zenith. Few who have taken this spiritual journey would say their lives have not been transformed. Mine was.

The back pouch contains provisions that are used by the pilgrim for his personal sustenance during the journey to Sabarimala and back.

Prasadam: Holy offering.

Karpoora Aarthi: Lamps lit with Camphor to show obeisance.

Sabari Peetam: The holy summit of Sabraimala.

Minimal bedding like blankets or bed sheets can also be carried. These can be used as a cushion for the head when we sleep on the ground.

Removing the Maala

The Sabarimala *Vrutham* ends only when the devotee returns home, lights a *Karpoora Arathi,* and then takes the *Prasadams*. The *Maala* has to be removed only after this, not at the *Sabari Peetam*.

The Six Shrines of Ayyappa – And their Significance

The pilgrim is supposed to visit all the six shrines before he embarks on the final leg of the trek up to Sabarimala. They are all located in different cities and locations and, except for the one on the Erumeli route, they are all connected by road and public transportation. Not all of these shrines are near or on the final route but form part of the overall legend. However, the pilgrim's journey is not considered complete until all six shrines have been visited. I always visit all six shrines, as is the custom and command.

1. Pandalam – The Royal Beginning

Kulathupuzhai: A village in the Kollam district of Kerala state, India. Also a tribute of the Kallada river.

Pandalam, in the Pathanamthita District in Kerala, is famous as the birthplace and home town of Lord Ayyappa. The place is perhaps the second only to Sabarimala in sanctity and significance. Pandalam is also the base camp from where scores of Swamis either proceed to Pamba for the shorter route or head to Erumeli to embark on the long trek to Sabarimala.

2. Achankovil - Home of Completeness

Though situated in the deep Kerala Forest, one can reach Achankovil only through Tamilnadu, winding through the traditional rural landscape which has been unchanged for centuries. Driving through the rich and dense forest route, we feel as if we are journeying back in time. The bliss permeating this town is palpable and we can feel its sublimity on each journey.

3. Aryankavu - Grove of Grace

The next temple on the journey is the Lord's third abode. Known in ancient days as Arya Vanam, the wooded temple of Aryankavu is 22 kilometres from Shenkottah bordering Tamilnadu. The Aryankavu Sastha Temple is a small, well-maintained temple built about 35 ft below the road level. Though located along the highway, the strategic location of the temple ensures that the mental peace of the devotees is protected from the sounds and vibrations of the outside world.

4. Kulathupuzhai - River of Peace

This shrine is situated amidst a forest range on the Thiruvananthapuram-Shenkottai Road that offers a dramatic panoramic view of the Kulathupuzhai Temple. It is located on the banks of Kulathu Puzha, a tributary of the Kallada River, and is in a reserve forest. The temple area is wide and big but the Sanctum complex is a very small but cool and quiet place.

5. Erumeli - Fort of Harmony

Erumeli is situated about 56 kilometres away from Kottayam town. This is the junction from where one starts his journey to Sabarimala. Ironically, the Lord who bestows peace is in the form of a fierce hunter here. But there is a great inner significance. This hunter kills not only the animals in the forest but also the inner animals in every spiritual aspirant. When this hunting happens, the Point of Awareness arises. Ego ceases - Reality presents itself as it is.

6. Sabarimala- Mount of Meditation

Moksha: The term for salvation in the Hindu tradition.

"Swamiyai Kandal Moksham Kittum": One obtains liberation when one attains the Darshan (holy sighting) at Sabarimala.

The most revered of all temples to Lord Sastha is the Dharma Sastha temple at Sabarimala. This sixth abode is situated in the midst of 18 hills, in a bowl of land.

Every year millions of devotees, irrespective of caste, creed or religion, throng the tiny complex to have *Darshan* of Lord Ayyappa. True to the Hindu philosophy of *Thathvamasi*, at Sabarimala the devotee communes directly with the Lord.

This hilly region surrounding Sabarimala has guarding deities in each of the hills. While intact and functioning temples exist at many places in surrounding areas (like Nilackal, Kalaketi, Inchiparakotta and Karimalai), remnants of old temples are also visible throughout the hills.

The *Pathinettampadi* or Holy 18 Steps that lead to the taking the Holy Darshan at the Sanctum Sanctorum of the Sabarimala Temple is considered an important privilege for every devotee. The steps represent the 18 stages one has to pass through to attain *Moksha*. The temple's magic is potent, its vibration ever powerful. *Swamiyai Kandal Moksham Kittum,* meaning salvation, is attained at Sabarimala.

ACE *Insights*   **5**

Understanding the Synergy of the Sabarimala Connection

Each year, people from different backgrounds, countries and cultures join me as we assemble together in the unique world that is Sabarimala.

What is it that draws us together?

What is this mysterious and invisible force that makes this attraction magnetic, almost irresistible?

For one thing, the mountain attracts us in such large numbers because of the compelling challenge it offers - the gratification of the climb itself and the ultimate reward at the summit.

The mountain expects a great deal from its climbers. If you don't have the discipline or focus to push through the rigours of fasting for nearly two months or undertake the arduous climb across five mountains, you will not hear Sabarimala's call. But for those of us who do hear it, the mountain's magical and magnetic spell holds us fast.

Synergy is a law of nature that states the following: A cohesive group is more than the sum of its parts.

Those who are drawn to that magic are, by their very nature, challenge seekers, conquerors and, eventually, victors. Furthermore, we are drawn together with the same purpose and so we gather energy and inspiration from each other's company. That too becomes part of the mountain's attraction.

When people have a united purpose, they are strongly attracted to each other and each one's journey is made easier by the presence of the others. Relationships are charged, enriched and strengthened when people become engaged in activities that naturally align with their core values and the mission at hand.

And when a hundred thousand challengers attempt to climb together, that can be as powerful, impressive and inspiring a force as any display of power nature can show us.

Canadian Geese and the Sabarimala trek

Canadian geese fly together in perfect synergy.

As the geese take flight from the Canadian shoreline, they lift off from the water in squawking discord. Yet, in a matter of seconds, a line begins to emerge from the mass of brown feathers. This line straightens, arches slightly and, then, as if on cue, bends sharply to form a perfect V shape.

The geese fly in V formation for a very pragmatic reason: a flock of geese flying in formation can move faster and maintain flight longer than any one goose flying alone. By flying in V formation, the whole flock adds at least 71% greater flying range than if each bird flew on its own.

Comparison: People who share a common direction and sense of community can get where they want to go more quickly and more easily when they are travelling together and taking on thrust from one another.

Whenever a goose falls out of formation, it suddenly feels the drag and resistance of trying to go it alone and quickly gets back into formation to take advantage of the lifting power of the bird immediately in front. To help that goose along, the geese behind him honk to encourage those up front to keep up their speed.

Comparison: It always makes more sense to form alliances with those who are heading in the same direction we are who can also send positive messages of encouragement to those ahead of them.

When a goose gets sick, is wounded or falls out, two geese fall out of formation and follow him down to help and protect him. They stay with him until he is either able to fly or has died. Then they launch out on their own or with another formation until they catch up with their group.

Comparison: We need to stand by each other, protect one another and sometimes make new alliances with those going in our direction.

Synergy is a dynamic form of leverage that helps us realize the value of others and encourages us to find the right people for our journey.

Your competitors can make the best allies

As I climb, I need to focus on what I am doing and how I can best keep up my stamina and focus. But, upon reflection, I always realize that it is my competitors who often make my best allies and help me attain my goal. They keep me honest, keep me on my toes and keep me motivated to improve.

Even though, at times in a competitive atmosphere, you can begin to feel dislike for those who seem to be having an easier time than you are in accomplishing the goals you are both striving for, rivalry can be a positive force.

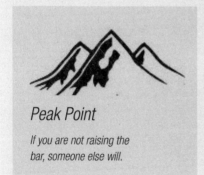

Peak Point

If you are not raising the bar, someone else will.

Without competition, we would probably get bored in that solitary and arduous physical exertion that it takes to accomplish the climb and we would have no comparative sign posts to encourage us to strive harder and do better.

We need our fellow climbers, all of whom are working toward the same goal we are, to reach our pinnacles of success.

On each of my trips, I come to realize that competitors can, at times, make the best allies.

MILESTONE

No Compromises - The Long Route

"Kallum Mullum Kaaluku Meddhai
Kundrum Kuzhiyum Kannuku Velicham"
["Stones and thorns will cushion our feet
Mounds and gorges will light the path"]

Verses from the Swamis' chants to inspire
climbers on the long Sabarimala trek

The journey begins

Swamiye Saranam Ayyappa!
Swamiye Saranam Ayyappa!!

Year after year, scores of worshippers of different castes, creeds and religions make their way to the holy mountain of Sabarimala chanting, "Swamiye Saranam Ayyappa."

In preparation

My *Viratham* begins on November 14th.

According to the rules of the Sabarimala pilgrimage, the Guruswamy is the supreme of all and I strictly follow my Guruswamy's instructions from the beginning of my fast until I return home after my pilgrimage.

On the day of departure, I take part in the ritual of *Irumudi Kettu* or *Kettu Nirai* in which I accept the *Irumudi*, my two-pouch head bag, from my Guruswamy.

Like all pilgrims, I carry my *Irumudi* with much devotion when I leave home. As is the custom, I neither bid goodbye to my loved ones nor look back since it is believed that once we start on our journey to Sabarimala, we are in the hands of the Lord himself.

When I leave home for Sabarimala, I break a coconut on a stone near my door step where a lit oil lamp will be placed.

The custom is that, until the pilgrim returns home after his pilgrimage, one of his family members will light this lamp at dusk each day and allow it to burn for a few of hours in a gesture of prayer for the well-being of the pilgrim and his safe return.

When they return home, all pilgrims will break a coconut on the same spot to signify the end of their pilgrimage. Then they will move on to the *Pooja* room to unload the *Irumudi* and remove the *Maala* which they have worn since the time of beginning the austerities. That signifies the last ritual of the pilgrimage.

Sabarimala Peruvazhi - The Trek

Since the pilgrimage to Sabarimala begins at the end of the severe 41-day fast, I have always successfully completed my fast on January 8th when I depart for New Delhi, India.

Canada has now been home for over a decade and I have become used to the vast expanse of the city, the uncluttered neighbourhoods, the sparse population and the orderly traffic (compared to India). Canada is proud of its well-organized systems, as it should be.

"Swamiye Saranam Ayyappa"

Holy chant: Translation: "Lord Ayyappa, give me shelter; take me under your wings."

But when I am thrown from the extreme of one culture to the other within a span of 24 hours, land in India and travel to one of the most congested areas of South India, I find myself in a totally different environment.

On January 11th each year, I arrive at the big city of Chennai and take part in the Coconut Rubbing function at the same Ayyappa Temple in Anna Nagar West where it all began 26 years ago. From Anna Nagar, I take an Auto Rickshaw to the Chennai Central Train Station and board the Trivandrum Mail at 8:00 p.m. headed for Kottayam in Kerala.

This is probably the lightest portion of my long trip as I am carrying only my *Irumudi* and my shoulder bag. The shoulder bag has in it only a few items of clothing, a few toiletries and, of course, a basic flashlight with 2 dry cells for illumination during the night trek through the Periyar Reserve which is populated by elephants and tigers.

On the morning of January 12th, I reach the city of Kottayam in the state of Kerala. Pilgrims must visit six particular shrines as part of the Sabarimala pilgrimage and, after refreshing in the men's washroom of the station, I take the city buses and private jeeps that transport pilgrims to the various Ayyappa shrines in adjacent cities which are all very close to each other.

The Three Routes to Sabarimala (0929 North 7706 East)

1. The Erumeli route is the most popular because it is believed that Ayyappa himself followed this path to the summit of Sabarimala and the route is dotted with shrines. It is also the most arduous as pilgrims must cover about 61 kilometres on foot through forest and hill paths. The Sabarimala trek cuts through leech-infested rain forests and hilly regions teeming with elephants and tigers. Without the strict observation of the prescribed penance, strong devotion, reasonable stamina and sound physique, it can be tough.

In spite of rapid modernization, the long route from Erumeli has been left untouched and all the tests the Swamis face, culminating in the all-fulfilling Darshanam at the Shrine, are still there.

What's more, the number of pilgrims converging here from around the world is actually increasing year by year.

2. The Vandiperiyar route starts at the 94.4 kilometres stone on the Kottayam – Kumily road through Changara Estate, Uppupaara and Paandithavalam.

3. The Chalakayam route is the easiest of all. Chalakayam is near the Pamba River which is the final destination and is considered as sacred as the Ganga. Devotees believe that a dip in the river can wash away the sins of a lifetime. The Sabarimala Sannidhanam is just 8 kilometres from here.

After visiting various Ayyappa temples along the way, I reach Erumeli in the evening. This is where the traditional trek to Sabarimala begins. Erumeli can be reached by road from Chengannur or Kottayam, towns that are well connected by trains.

ERUMELI

12th January – 19.00 Hours

Erumeli is a small town in Kottayam district about 56 kilometres from the main city. It is known as the place of communal amity where three religions - Christianity, Hindi and Islam - coexist. It is particularly renowned for the shrines to Lord Dharmasastha and Vavar Swamy (the Muslim lieutenant of Lord Ayyappa) that exist on the same street facing each other – a rare sight anywhere in the world today. [*See picture*].

Here, in this small town in Western Kerala, members of two communities have managed, through legend, lore and ritual, to create a shared spiritual and social space and have bridged what many claim is an insurmountable divide. The Sabarimala pilgrimage, in the course of about 40 days, will bring nearly 50 million pilgrims through this town.

The pilgrims visit both shrines to worship before commencing their journey. The 70 kilometre trek from Erumeli to the mountaintop shrine of the god Ayyappa at Sabarimala cannot be completed without first paying respects to his friend the Muslim pirate/saint Vavar and asking his permission to proceed. At the Vavar Mosque, we worship at the shrine and *Vibhuthi* is given to the devotees as *Prasadam*.

The pilgrims then bathe in the nearby pond. A refreshing bath in cold waters renews one's energy and prepares one for the rigorous walk.

After filling the holy coconut with ghee and packing it and the other essentials for offerings to Lord Ayyappa in the *Irumudi,* the Guru places the sacred *Irumudi* on my head, as all the Gurus do for all the pilgrims, while we chant *Saranam*. Like all the pilgrims, I leave each place without looking at anyone or bidding goodbye to family or friends. It is by following such a strict discipline, walking barefoot all the way till the end, that the pilgrim will realize his Self and attain Lord Ayyappa.

My belief is rock solid because, each year for over 26 years at Erumeli, I see the power and passion with my own eyes, hear it all with my own ears and feel it within my own body and soul.

When I arrive at Erumeli, I am struck by the festival-like atmosphere that pervades the streets. Coming from Canada, I am used to a little sobriety but here the air above the town is filled with shouts, chants, ecstatic cries and the chatter of the thousands who fill the streets, restaurants and shops of this otherwise nondescript town.

Pilgrims wear coloured balloons, paint their faces, beat drums and dance. In front of me, hundreds of paint-smeared, ecstatic men dance, prance and sing their way around the large, pink mosque and then make their way across the street to the Hindu Dharmasastha Temple. A continuous line of bodies creates an umbilical cord between the temple and the mosque. The sound of their songs and the rhythm of their dances suggest a living connection transforming the two distinctly separate spaces into one. Hundreds more stream down from the bus stand towards the mosque and the temple that sits across from it.

This celebration marks the victory of Lord Ayyappa over the evil demon Mahishi. Legend has it that the tribes of Erumeli helped Lord Ayyappa win the battle over Mahishi. And so people coming here are supposed to dress and dance like tribals. The devotees perform a group tribal dance called *Petta Thullal* covering a distance of about half a kilometre. In olden days, tribals celebrated God Sastha as their guardian deity and believed that the welfare of their tribe was His concern. These tribal dance forms are incorporated into today's Petta Thullal.

Pettai: Area and Thullal: Dance.

Peruvazhi: The long 56 kilometre route through the jungles and mountains to the temple.

Doing this dance before embarking upon their journey enables the devotees to give up their egos and realize that everyone is equal in front of Lord Ayyappa.

Finally, the temple is visited again to seek authorization from Lord Ayyappa to tread the sacred hill *Sabari*.

Then the pilgrims leave Erumeli under the guidance of their Guruswamy for Sannidhanam. The *Peruvazhi* to the temple starts here and the lengthy, barefoot walk in the forests through night and day is a wonderful experience.

I leave Erumeli by 8 p.m. to start my trek and walk for four hours straight in order to reach the base of the first mountain by midnight.

Murali Murthy

At Erumeli, the significance of the Lord takes the form of a hunter. This hunter kills not only the animals in the forest but also the inner animals in every spiritual aspirant. This hunt allows the Point of Awareness to arise. Ego ceases and reality presents itself as it is.

PERUR THODU

12th January – 21.00 Hours

The Perur Thodu is a river bank about 4 kilometres from Erumeli. It is from here the rise begins. Giving alms here is important. By giving alms, one is disposing of all *Dharma* and seeking asylum in Ayyappa.

Dharma is a concept of central importance in Indian philosophy and religion. It means the Natural Law. As well as referring to Law in the universal or abstract sense, Dharma designates those behaviours considered necessary for the maintenance of the natural order of things such as duty, vocation, religion and all behaviour considered appropriate, correct or morally upright.

Thodu: Stream.

The forest beyond Perur Thodu is Poongavanam (Ayyappa's garden) and the 4 kilometres walk through this very dense forest is wonderful. It is the evening and therefore dark but it seems dark even in the afternoon as the trees are huge, thin and tall so the sunlight hardly touches the surface of the mountain.

We walk on a proper road for about 3-4 kilometres from the starting point which abuts many rubber estates. Then we are on the plains and reach a small stream, Perur Thodu. It is believed that Lord Ayyappa rested here on his way to Sabarimala and so pilgrims offer *Pori* to the fishes here.

Lord Ayyappa's Garden starts from this place and from here the walk is through many undulating hills.

KAALAKETTI

13th January – 01.00 Hours

Though we are trekking throughout the night, we are accompanied by the music and the dancing of the high-spirited devotees as we climb and this makes us forget our lack of sleep and tiredness.

About 10 kilometres from Perur Thodu is Kaalaketti. There is a shrine here where the pilgrims light camphor and break coconuts.

AZHUDHA RIVER

13th January – 02.00 Hours

The sacred river of Azhudha, a tributary of the Pamba, is about 2 kilometres down from Kaalaketti. Pilgrims rest on the banks of the Azhudha, bathing in the river before proceeding because, on the other side of the river is the steep Azhudha hill, famous for its arduous track. Before we leave, we also take a pebble from this river, and carry it with us so we can offer it at Kallidum Kunru, which is at the summit of the Azhudha hill.

Peak Point

Work from your strengths, not from your weaknesses.

Some of us are continuing on while others decide to camp here for the night. I admire the resilience of those who carry on despite the hour and the fatigue but I have made good time so I decide to take time to pause and rest. I will still meet my deadline if I continue to pace myself and cover my journey at my intended speed.

I take the opportunity to revel in the cool breeze up here in the mountains. For me, the mountains are synonyms with bliss. When I am there, there is nothing to distract me and I am overcome by the amazing beauty of nature. But fatigue is catching up with us all and each one of us looks for the nearest makeshift

Murali Murthy

tent or a log to lie down and stretch out our legs. We are so tired that it doesn't matter where we catch a few moments of sleep.

The first day of the trek

As I lie down for the night at Azhudha, I reflect back on the first day of the trek and the experiences of that day.

What have I learned on my first day?
When things aren't easy and you do them anyway, you learn new things.
Bounce back often and faster. Keep going.

AZHUDHA MOUNTAIN BASE

13th January – 07.00 Hours

I awake at 6 a.m. and freshen up by bathing in the Azhudha River. It is going to be a big day and the more ground I cover before the sun starts smiling down on me, the better it is going to be.

The Azhudha mountain, which begins here, is steeper to climb and as we move upwards, we have to rest often to take a breath and sing devotional songs.As I write this, I reflect on and understand why singing these devotional songs has become more enjoyable each year.

The ambience that is created when masses of people are chanting 'Swamiye Saranam Ayyappa' together is utterly moving. Devotion simply pours out of these songs and the words of prayer. I think that is another reason why people make such a pilgrimage together in large numbers. We become one, selfless and wishing to help the others complete this journey successfully. Devotion can never be enforced on anyone – it must always come from within and, in the two kilometres of steep ascent, there are very few who do not shed a few tears.

Taking each step of the climb and enjoying every moment immersed in devotion helps us realize our goal and focus on the priorities in life.

KALLIDUM KUNRU

13th January – 10.00 Hours

At the summit of Azhudha is Kallidum Kunnu. Here we drop the pebbles that we have been carrying from the Azhudha River. This gesture marks the defeat of Mahishi, just as Lord Ayyappa threw huge stones on Mahishi to bury her after defeating her to ensure that she does not rise again.

At the summit of Kallidum Kunru, I take a short break, just long enough to soothe my nerves from the heightened emotions of the climb and give my feet a well deserved rest.

AZHUDHA UCHI (PEAK)

13th January – 08.00 Hours

After another steep climb, we reach the peak of the Azhudha *Uchi* which is called Injipparakkotta or Udumbara Mala. There is a small Ayyappa temple here and another small shrine to Udumbara, a forest God, where devotees offer worship by lighting camphor.

It is here where we also perfom *Vedi Vazhipaadu*, the ritual of burning firecrackers in the name of the devotee. This tradition is followed in many places along the way because the noise of the crackers keeps wild animals away.

As I trek, I hear the continuous chanting of *'Swamiye Saranam Ayyappa! Swamiye Saranam Ayyappa!'*

Azhudha is the common name for the river and the mountain. Azhudha River is a tributary of Pamba River and Azhudha Mountain is the first of the steep mountains en route to Sabarimala.

The loud chants break the ear-piercing silence of the forests. The fervor and zeal of the pilgrims as they sing is absolutely consuming. The pilgrims are so involved in their communion with the God that all the hardship, the exhaustion of the journey and the long trek still ahead do not really register. All that matters is reaching the spiritual place beyond the realm of matter.

As I look up towards the Azhudha, I can see the long, steady march ahead of me. But, as droplets of sweat fall from me to earth like rain, I fall into a kind of trance. I only know the next step, and the next step, and the next step.

By about three or four o'clock my heartbeat begins to change. At first it is minimal, a gentle pounding that seems faster than normal. Gradually it grows louder.

It is the altitude. I have never been this high in my life When at last we made the peak, just as dawn cracked over the horizon, a sense of accomplishment burst upon my being. Cold and exhausted, but ecstatic with joy, I knew I had pushed myself beyond anything before. It was a personal feat.

On my first climb, 26 years ago, I had never been this high before in my life so it was frightening and new. But now I am a veteran and know what to do. I slow my pace, placing each foot but a few inches in front of the other, to regulate my breathing and be conscious of the changes.

We reach the peak just as dawn cracks over the horizon and a great sense of accomplishment bursts upon my being. I am cold and exhausted but ecstatic with joy at the same time. I know I have pushed myself farther than ever before. It is a personal victory.

INCHIPPARAKOTA

13th January – 11.00 Hours

The next important milestone is Inchipparakota. Here again, pilgrims offer prayers and break coconuts before we carefully begin the slippery descent along the path down to Karimalai Thodu.

We rest there for a while, taking in the sight of Azhudha Hill which we have already climbed on one side and Karimalai Hill on the other.

Uchi: Peak.

Aazhi: Fire.

Then we begin to climb again and I watch with appreciation as total strangers come forward to help others climb up. The synergy and team support of each person supporting the other, holding an arm, pushing someone up and offering words of encouragement, is so reassuring. We are all doing all we can to help each other reach our common goal.

MUKKUZHI

13th January – 12.00 Hours

Along our next descent there is a place called Mukkuzhi where there are small shrines to various gods. We stop there to offer worship and then continue further down to a valley at the foothill of Karimalaii.

KARI VALAM THODU

13th January – 14.00 Hours

In the valley between Azhudha and Karimalaii flows a stream where many elephants from the forest congregate to quench their thirst. This place is called Kari Valam Thodu. We take another short break here and I brace myself to climb the big one – the imposing, almighty Karimalai.

Karimalai

13th January – 15.00 Hours

The lengthy five kilometre climb on Karimalaii is the most difficult part of the trek. Karimalaii has about seven levels to cross which are climbed in stages before reaching the peak. Pilgrims light the *Aazhi* to protect themselves from elephants and other wild animals and the cold weather.

As the ascent is extremely difficult, the pilgrims continuously chant *Saranams* to inspire them along their journey.

For a moment as I climb, just a brief moment, I feel the physical strain and pause to look at those walking briskly past me. Seeing them rejuvenates me and, in no time, I join the throng in our common trek and am climbing with them, matching step for step.

Yes, I admit it – there are times when I am tempted to give it all up and look for the nearest winding detour. In these moments I want to escape to the nearest hamlet, hire a Jeep and pay the driver a king's ransom to drive me to Pamba. But when I look at people to my left and to my right who are still climbing, people behind and ahead of me who continue to climb in spite of the same challenges I face, I know I cannot be weak. Seeing their strength is enough motivation for me to continue the climb.

Just one more step, then another and the next one and I know I too will make it.

It takes hours to climb the entire hill and reach the top. In certain sections, the path is very narrow and only one person can walk it at a time. On one side there is mountain rock and on the other side there is a steep fall with huge trees. This route is treacherous as elephant and tiger sightings are common which adds a new dimension to the physically difficult climb.

To make matters all the more difficult, the mound near the peak is so steep to climb that pilgrims constantly chant the name of the Lord to help them reach the top.

There are many stories that have been told about this place. It is said that there are forest Gods and Goddess who protect this forest and also the people who pass through it. In the *Saranam vili* they also mention and thank them.

All around me people are chanting The Ayyappa Varavu verses which I find very significant. "*Panai pole randu kaallum, Parrai pole randu muttum" [On the one side is the steep valley and on the other side are the huge trees and imposing rocks.].* And as we climb higher, the visibility on the path is impaired by the dense fog. Now we all have to use small torches to see where we are going.

The competition is great as we near the summit and this competition keeps us all working hard to reach our goal of reaching the mountain top. On each of my trips, especially at times like these, I come to realize that competitors can also, at times, make the best allies.

As I continue my stride, I notice that, while it is dark and shady on the path because of the tall trees, the leaves on the tallest treetops glitter with a different colour - they are the ones that get the sunlight first. As in life, so it is on the Sabarimala climb. The ones who make it to the top first achieve the brightest and warmest light.

Finally, I reach the top of Karimalai and its flat terrain is the perfect place to rest.

Karimalai - The descent

In some ways, the descent from Karimalai is a whole new experience but, in many other ways, it is still similar. To begin with, there are stones and thorns everywhere. If it is raining or has just rained, something that happens a lot in this region, the slopes become very slippery, adding treachery to the difficulty of walking barefoot among stones and thorns, particularly as we have to carefully balance the *Irumudi* on our heads. If we lose focus for even a nanosecond, it is the perfect recipe for disaster.

Aazhi - The campfire lit by the pilgrims to generate heat in the biting cold and to ward off the elephants and tigers lurking nearby.

Karivalan Thodu: Kari means elephant and Valam means wander.

Vana Devatamaar: Forest gods, Vana Devimaar: Forest goddesses. "Panai pole randu kaallum, Parrai pole randu muttum": Translation: "On the one side is the steep valley and on the other side are the huge trees and imposing rocks."

"Kallum mullum kaaluku methai, kundrum kuzhiyum kannuku velicham", Translation: "Stones and thorns will cushion the feet and mounds and gorges will show the way."

To help us on this difficult decline, we continually recite a popular chant to motivate the climbers. *"Kallum mullum kaaluku methai, kundrum kuzhiyum kannuku velicham." [Stones and thorns will cushion the feet and mounds and gorges will show the way.]*

It is precisely this uncompromising, make-no-excuses attitude demonstrated in the chants that makes us stronger and gives us the power and energy to move on.

It is what helped me on one particular climb when I slipped on the wet ground and received a large gash on my foot. It was bleeding profusely but I could not afford to stop and tend it if I wanted to reach my destination before dark. I knew I would have to wait till the next day to reach the dispensary at Pampa. I tied a sheet around the wound to temporarily stop the bleeding and simply carried on.

Finally, after what seems like eons, I make it to the base of Karimalai. I am now on the other side – very close to the holy river Pamba, now only 5 kilometres away. Pilgrims rest and worship the local deities before proceeding.

PERI YAANAI VATTAM

13th January – 18.00 Hours

Now a more strenuous descent begins with rocks and huge trees hurdling across the path. After about 3 kilometres of walking, we come to Peri Yaanai Vattam. This is the base of Karimalai and camping grounds on the banks of the Pamba River. One can get a good sight of Makara Jyothi from here.

SIRI YAANAI VATTAM

13th January – 20.00 Hours

One more kilometre of walking and we reach Siri Yaanai Vattam, the starting point of the Karimalai descent. The downward path is renowned for its boulders, rocks and huge trees.

Pilgrims take out the provisions they have been carrying on the back portion of their *Irumudi* and prepare food here. They also feed many other fellow pilgrims. In the Ayyappa cult, *Annadhaanam* is an important tradition.

PAMBA NADI

13th January – 21.00 Hours

The Pamba River is at the base of Sabarimala and the third longest river in the South Indian state of Kerala and the longest river in the princely state of Travancore. Pampa is the most important and holiest spot on the way to

Sannidhanam because the Sabarimala temple is located on its banks. Perhaps even more importantly, the Pamba River is considered as holy as the Ganges and it is acknowledged that its waters purify one from curse and evil.

Still, many pilgrims feel that Pamba is too crowded and prefer to stay at Peri Yaanai Vattam or Siri Yaanai Vattam rather than go on to the Pamba River even though one can reach the banks of the holy Pamba River in about a kilometre from those two sites. But I prefer to continue on and walk for close to three hours through the forest to reach the holy Pamba.

When I reach Pamba, I am speechless as I stand at the foot of Sabarimala looking up at the sheer size of the mountain range I have just crossed. Surrounded by rivers, lush trees and majestic mountains, the Sabarimala peaks invite me. Tomorrow morning we will climb the Holy 18 Steps to the Sabarimala Temple.

PAMBA ANNADHANAM

13th January – 22.00 Hours

Viri: The area of makeshift tents set up by the All India Ayyappa Seva Sangam.
Dolis: Special carry chairs available at Pamba, custom designed for the physically indisposed or challenged who will be carried up to the shrine by 4 people.

Vilakku: Lights.

Papad: A thin, crispy Indian preparation sometimes described as a cracker or flatbread.

At Pamba, *Viri* have been set up in the forest for people to rest in the evening. There is also a guest house and other accommodation options, restaurants, tea shops, shops selling religious paraphernalia and chemists as well.

There are also *Dolis* available at Pamba for the physically disabled to be carried up to the shrine.

At various places, I can also see *Annadhaanam* taking place. People are cooking and feeding others as well. This is called *Pamba Sadhya*. The Pamba feast and the decorating and floating of lamps are important rituals followed at the bank of the Pamba river.

Thousands of pilgrims are fed at Pamba and groups of pilgrims are preparing feasts with the provisions that have been carried in their *Irumudi*. When a group of pilgrims is ready to feed their fellow pilgrims, they display a large *Papad* outside their cottage. It is usually

Peri Yaaynai Vattam: The big meeting place for elephants.

Siri Yaanai Vattam: The small meeting place for elephants.

Annadhaanam: Free feeding.

Nadi: River.

the Kanniswamy who are fed first, as they are considered to be Lord Ayyappa himself. After the feast, the Guruswamy is honoured by pilgrims prostrating before him and offering him the Guruswamy Dakshina.

PAMBA VILAKKU

13th January – 23.00 Hours

At sunset, the pilgrims decorate lamps of various shapes made out of bamboo from the forest. They carry these lamps from their *Viri* up to Pamba and float them on the River. This is called *Pamba Vilakku*. It is an awesome sight to watch so many lamps floating on the river in the dark.

Tomorrow is the 14th of January and when we will all celebrate Makara Sankranti.

It is the big day. From Pamba, the tough 6 kilometres trek up to the Sabarimala shrine culminates in the Holy 18 Steps, locally called the Pathinettampadi. This is a flight of steps that lead up to the shrine where pilgrims are rewarded with the final *Darshan* – sighting of the deity.

This is the day I have been waiting for - the ascent to Sabarimala.

ACE *Insights*   **6**

Reflections on the Night of January 12th

Peak Point

Never say, "I can't do this."

Your body will faithfully reciprocate that fear.

Always talk positively.

Any of life's challenges aren't that different from ascending steep mountains. Sometimes the path is difficult – hot air blowing on you; no hand rails; no lights; definitely no medical help - but you keep going because the beauty of the amazing vistas awaiting you at the final destination is made up of all the steps you take to reach it on the steep ascents along the way.

Take it one step at a time. There's only one way from Point A to Point B. You start moving and then keep going.

How to accomplish your goal

Be flexible

Let go of the need to be on solid ground. Sometimes life is like walking on unstable terrain that crumbles and is jagged. But it is also beautiful and the path that will lead you to your final destination.

Appreciate the beauty and go with the flow by opening yourself up to new ways of moving forward, even if it means being a bit wobbly for a while.

Take breaks

The climb to the top isn't a race. If you need nourishment – mentally or physically – stop and take a break to drink, have a quick snack or catch your breath. Encourage yourself by thinking about how far you've come.

Think of the lovely rocks that doubled as stone benches where you took a moment to sit when your body begged for reprieve. And there's nothing like a hot cup of tea or a cold juice to say climbing Sabarimala was a worthwhile experience.

The pursuit of life's big goals can feel long and exhaustive. Take breaks when you need them because they rejuvenate you. Add in elements of fun to any difficult journey. It makes the experience more enjoyable and the memories sweeter.

Have a guide

Rely on someone to help you when the going gets tough. Having my Guruswamy as a guide in the first year was a comfort and a motivation. His coaching made reaching the top easier for me than if I had tried to do it on my own.

When you are in an unknown and sometimes dangerous territory, having someone you trust to lead the way is a comfort and a necessity.

Take calculated risks

Each year, there are cases of a few people getting trampled by wild elephants. The Periyar Reserve is the elephants' domain and we must never forget that we are entering their territory *[See the pictures attached]*. So we must be cautious. As a rule, we travel in groups and chant in unison to keep them away. If it's night time, we walk with lit torches. Always have the right tools with you to make sure you are safe.

Risk what you must but be careful not to risk too much.

Encourage others

Offer and receive encouragement to those climbing the same mountain. The sense of community among the climbers on the Sabarimala trek, is awe-inspiring.

For example, it is customary for people descending a mountain to blow their towel cloths at the people on their way up. This gesture creates a breeze to cool the climbers as they sweat on the way up. Those on the way down also offer Glucose powder, refreshments and water to those still striving for the top. Most importantly, they offer assurance to those still struggling that the top is within reach.

On my way up, I really appreciate the help from total strangers and I make sure that I pay it forward on my way down.

Let others in. Don't underestimate their courage and strength. Rely on them to buoy you up during the difficult times and return the favour, providing strength and encouragement when they need it.

Reward yourself

These are my three rewards on my trips to Sabarimala.

The breathtaking view from the top.
The tremendous sense of accomplishment.
The undeniable health benefits.

Yes, I sweated and panted but I took breaks too.

I wondered if the top really existed as my legs ached but when I stopped to appreciate the breathtaking views, it was all worth it.

Accomplishing goals are inherently rewarding in themselves but there is also nothing wrong with actually rewarding yourself. And as is often the case with challenges, once they're completed, we realize they seemed a lot harder at the beginning than they actually were.

Reflections on the Night of January 13th

Like any journey of significance, themes emerge. Somewhere beyond the peaks of Sabarimala, I learn and relearn some lessons that resonate beyond the mountain-climbing task at hand.

Sometimes, your greatest competitor is the one inside your head

The challenge, I think, may not be man vs. mountain. It most definitely is you vs. yourself.

Peak Point

Before physical momentum comes mental momentum.

On the way up, it is easy to let the anxiety demons stop you in your tracks.

"I'm not going to make it. I'm not strong enough."

These fears take over during the day and, if you're not careful, they can soon sap precious mental and physical energy.

You must overcome their chorus to get to the top.

You can't let the voices of panic and the ghosts of past failures cloud your climb to success. Training and mental power help put the demons in their place.

Perseverance is a beautiful thing

Sabarimala may be a high summit but neither mountain peaks nor tenure assure fulfillment. The last lesson from the mountains might be that it is the effort itself, not the achievement of the summit, that brings satisfaction.

One acquires experience through technical skills but true success depends on emotional resilience and communication skills.

Appreciate the journey

Always look forward but, occasionally, look back to know where you've been. That way you can appreciate the beauty of where you stand.

One step at a time

Especially on the steep, narrow Karimalai descent, I have had to caution myself not to hurry, to focus and take it one step at a time.

In both the ascent and the descent of the climb, the plodding may seem tedious but there's good reason for this. A slow but deliberate pace is the key to continually managing energy and acclimatizing to altitude.

Discipline is the single greatest key to the enjoyment of climbing and the satisfaction of summiting Sabarimala.

On the mountain, this means taking extra time, if you feel you need to, or taking short hikes to higher elevation at the end of each stretch and then coming back down. The idea is to take a taste of the thinner air that awaits you and return to a comfortable place so you can sleep at night. That way, you will be better equipped, mentally and physically, to take on the challenge in the morning.

Peak Point

If you are brought to a problem, you will be brought through the problem.

Life is always about movement from one comfort zone to the next. Give yourself time and room to adjust along the way.

One foot in front of the other. Slowly but surely and deliberately – all the way to the top.

That is the best way to ensure you reach your goals.

Be confident but don't underestimate the task at hand

I still haven't reached the Sabarimala summit but I have covered the bulk of the climb. So, obviously, the Erumeli to Pamba climb is doable but not to be underestimated. Although it is not a technical climb, ascending to that height in less than two days is no easy feat.

There is a fine balance between confidence and underestimating the task ahead. Don't be dissuaded from tackling a daunting project but be realistic and know that it may take more energy and determination than you had bargained for.

Departing from chilly Toronto, Canada.

Arriving in warm Chennai, India.

Alighting from the train in Kerala, India.

In Kottayam, Kerala, ready for the trek.

Erumeli - starting point for the trek, a congruence of many
cultures - where Hunduism and Islam exist side by side.

At Erumeli - ready for the trek.

Friends made on the trek.

Early morning - the trek.

Passing a tea estate along the way.

The cool Azhudha river stream.

Sweating it out - on the trek.

Braving it in the sweltering sun.

The trek can get lonely at times.

An elephant calf seen on the way.

Warning signs.

Warning signs - reinforced.

At the base of Azhudha - Hill 1 - crossing a treacherous slippery stream.

Braving it out in the heat.

While walking barefoot, the sand can be pretty hot too.

Tired but resilient.

A steady stream of pilgrims.

Aah cool shades.

Cool shaded area.

Finally, relief.

Sighting the final peak - still a long way to go.

Crossing one more stream.

Taking a short break.

The treacherous Karimala descent - a typical rock-filled trail.

Scorching heat.

A rest area on Neelimalai - the final frontier.

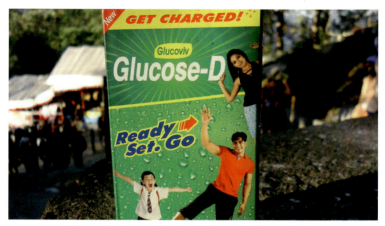

The trekker's true friend - A Glucose D Energy Pack.

The Sabarimala Sannidhanam, the final summit.

MILESTONE

The Last Frontier - At the Peak

*"Travelers will cross many rivers and climb many mountains.
Plainsmen may always live within a valley.
But only those seeking truth will ever reach the summit."*

11th century Indian saying

THE FINAL CLIMB: PAMBA TO SABARIMALA

14th January – 06.00 Hours

I have spent the night at the Viri – the makeshift tent – and wake up at 6:00 a.m. refreshed from the good night's sleep. I am among the first people to bathe in the ice-cold, pristine water of the Pamba River which rushes around me at great speed.

Pure in every sense!

PAMBA TO SABARIMALA

14th January – 07.00 Hours

When I begin my march towards Sannidhanam, the top of Sabarimala, I am joined by scores of pilgrims who had chosen to take the Chinna Paadhai (the shorter route), and have reached Pamba by road. From here, it is a steep climb of about 6 km.

The first point of worship on the climb up is the Kanni Moola Ganapathi Temple and pilgrims mark their arrival at this temple by breaking a coconut.

Then we continue on until we come to a small shrine meant for Pandala Raja, the King of Pandala. According to legend, since Lord Ayyappa comes from the Pandala Dynasty, whoever visits the Lord has to obtain permission from the king or his representative here. *Vibhuthi* is given to the pilgrims as *Prasadam* by the Pandala Raja's representatives.

NEELIMALAI

14th January – 08.00 Hours

I reach the foot of Neelimalai, the point where the steep trek begins, and see there is a slight fog cover. On either side of the path there is dense forest with huge trees and wild bushes.

As I stand at the foot hill of Neelimalai, I can see that it is much steeper than all the other hills around here. Though there are stone steps and many resting places, one has to work hard to climb Neelimalai.

In fact, cardiac patients are advised not to take this trek and there are cardiac clinics along the way for emergencies. Also, in the last few years, many oxygen parlours have been set up for people who have problems breathing.

Just a few short steps into the trek, it suddenly strikes me. For a while now, I have been hearing a song and its lyrics suddenly take on a new meaning for me. "*Neelimalai Yetram kadinam kadinam*", the Neelimala climb is tough indeed.

While climbing this mountain, the pilgrims constantly chant: "*Yendhividappa Thookkividappa.*"

"*Swamiye Saranam Ayyappa! Swamiye Saranam Ayyappa!*"

The loud chants break the pristine silence of the forests and the fervour and zeal of the pilgrims are shattering. Absolutely consuming. Each one of us is so caught up in our communion with the God that none of the hardships and exhaustion of the long trek matter.

At times like this I am again reminded that climbing a mountain is indeed a metaphor for life. As I focus on taking just one more step upwards, Neelimalai reminds me to see into the deeper meaning of my journey.

APPAACHIMEDU

14th January – 09.00 Hours

When I reach Appaachimedu, about 3 kilometres from Sannidhanam, I see people throwing small rice flour balls into the forest at a place called Ippaachikkuzhi, which is next to Appaachimedu. This is believed to be the spot where the offering was made to the Vana Devathas.

In a few metres, I reach Sabari Peetam. This place has a special mention in the Indian epic Ramayana. It is where an old lady named Sabari resided. Sri Rama, on his way to Sri Lanka, visited Sabari at this place and blessed her. Pilgrims worship Sabari here and proceed.

"Yendhividappa Thookkividappa": "God! Pick me up. Lift me up." Vana Devathas: The mythological Godly guardians of the forest.

Aalamaram: Banyan Tree.
Saram Kuthi: a small arrow made of bamboo, affixed by first timers to a Banyan tree to inform of their arrival.

The next stop is Saram Kuthi Aal where there is a huge *Aalamaram*. On my first trip, I brought *Saram Kuthi* here and affixed it to the tree. Now, I perform the Saram Kuthi every time I come.

Finally, I reach the tip of holy Sabarimala and find the mountain to be abuzz with activity and yet so peaceful at the same time. There is a rare breed of monkeys swinging from branch to branch and birds chirping very loudly from the huge, looming trees.

I have never seen these kinds of birds here before. They are very beautiful with white-striped bodies and long tails. Their melodious chirping is a song.

The view from the summit is something that I have never seen, imagined or experienced before. The sky is lit in several shades of orange, blue and purple and the spectacular vista before me is unbelievable. The view of the surrounding mountain range is spectacular as the panorama of hills and smaller mountain peaks gleam in the riot of colour. For the first time, I know what it means to have a breathtaking experience.

Although every inch of my body is in pain, the sense of accomplishment I feel and the scene in front of me is worth every second of hardship I have experienced getting here.

Surrounded by the wide open sky, the complete silence and spectacular mountains, I stand atop Sabarimala awestruck by nature's beauty.

The Karpoora Aazhi

Near the Sannidhaanam is the Karpoora Aazhi, a bonfire of camphor and coconuts that is lit when the season begins in Mid-November and burns constantly until the end of the season in Mid-January. Thousands of coconuts burn here day and night. It is said that the smoke coming from the fire, in which so many ghee-soaked coconuts burn, cleanses the whole atmosphere.

I now offer the ghee I have carried inside my coconut to the Lord as *Abishegam*. I take the ghee out of the broken coconut and throw it on the hearth of Karpoora Aazhi to join the other offerings being burnt there.

The Significance of the Padhinettam Padi

There are 18 mountains surrounding Sabarimala and each one is represented by one step of the Holy 18 Steps. You cannot step onto the Padinettam Padi without *Vrutham* in Sabarimala because, by climbing the steps, you are actually stepping into the zone of a particular Devata who guards it and only if you have the *Virutha Balam* do you qualify to be blessed.

Karpoora Aazhi: A bonfire of camphor and coconuts.

Devata: Gods.

Padinettam Padi: The Holy 18 Steps.

There are many myths associated with the holy Padhinettam Padi. Some believe the 18 steps represent the 18 divine forces guarding the Sabarimala Zone. By climbing these steps, we are actually stepping into the zone of the deity. So only our *Virutham* or fasting has given us the strength to cross over the Holy 18 Steps.

These steps are also figuratively called Ponnu Padhinettam Padi, [Golden 18 Steps], *Ponnu* being an epithet to denote the holy touch of the Lord's feet. But the *Ponnu* has now become literal because the steps have been covered with gold.

Still others believe that the first five steps denote the *Indriyas*, eyes, ears, nose, tongue and skin. The next eight steps signify the *Ragas*, Tatwa, Kama, Krodha, Moha, Lobha, Madha, Mastraya and Ahamkara and the next three steps signify the *Gunas*, Satwa, Rajas and Thamas. The 17th and the 18th denote *Vidhya* and *Jeevathma Bhava*, intelligence and life knowledge.

Those who climb all these steps are believed to achieve *Punya Darshan*.

In order to enter the Sabarimala Temple, the pilgrim must climb the Holy 18 Steps and, before ascending or descending the steps, pilgrims break coconuts as offerings to the steps.

Only pilgrims wearing the *Irumudi* on their heads are allowed to ascend the steps. The steps can be used only twice – once to ascend for the *Darshan* and then again before leaving after the *Darshan*. Even while descending, pilgrims must carry the empty *Irumudi* on their heads.

At the foot of Padhinettam Padi, I can see the small shrines of Kadutha Swami and Karuppa Swami who serve as *Dwarapaalakas* on either side. Adjacent to these shrines, pilgrims break coconuts before ascending the Holy 18 Steps.

We raise slogans and chant, "Swamiye Saranam Ayyappa" as we ascend the steps, bowing to each step.

Once we climb the steps with the *Irumudi* and we experience the Holy Sighting, *Darshan*, communing with DharmaSastha, another name for the Lord. It is believed that we have reached the pinnacle of our destination. Our goal is accomplished even though the *Nei Abhishekam* is our next task.

Darshan is the Sanskrit term that means meeting God or Holy Sighting. It is the essential moment in which a devotee communes directly with the divine. Throughout India, the day begins with a prayer acknowledging the divine in its innumerable forms.

Dwarapaalakas: Entrance Guards.

Nei Abhishekam: Ghee Offering.

After the *Darshan*, I follow the other devotees to perform the traditional breaking of coconuts which we have all brought with us on the journey and offer the ghee inside to the Lord for *Abishegam*.

The *Sannidhaanam* is located above the Holy 18 Steps at a height of 40 ft amidst the serenity of the forests and hills. This ancient sanctum was rebuilt after a fire in 1950 and the original stone idol of the Lord was replaced by a new idol made of *Panchaloha* (5 metals) in which the Lord is seen in a meditating posture with a smiling face, blessing his devotees. A huge *Dwajasthambha* stands in front of the temple.

I enter the Temple and my first glimpse of Lord Ayyappa is incredible and dazzling. I feel as if something pleasant has been poured onto my face. My whole body involuntarily sways slightly backwards. It is a wonderful feeling; a feeling of happiness and peace.

MAKARA SANKRANTI DAY - 14th January

January 14th is Makara Sankranti Day, the day when the Lord Ayyappa is adorned with jewels and we celebrate the divine lights that signal the end of our pilgrimage. Every year without fail, miraculous events occur on this very special day.

MAKARA JYOTI

In the evening, the stage is set for the Makara Jyoti. Devotees can view the *Makara Jyothi* from nine places in and around Sannidhanam. They are Sannidhanam, Pandithavalam, Pulmedu, Saramkuthi, Neelimala, Marakootam, Hilltop, Chalakayam, and Attathodu.

> *Makara Jyoti: Effulgence, radiant splendour.*
>
> *Sannidhaanam: The ancient sanctum or Temple.*
>
> *Dwajasthambha: Flag staff.*

All the devotees are excited and occupy appropriate places to view the spectacle on the top of Kaandamala (a mountain to the east and exactly facing Sannidhanam). We click photos of each other and in groups. The whole of Sabarimala is abuzz with only one sound – "*Saranam Ayyappa*". We look with eagerness at the sky, searching for Makara Jyoti.

Firstly, *Thiruvaabaranam* for the Lord are transported from the Old Pandalam Palace to Sabarimala. At 6:30 p.m., the *Thiruvabharnam* arrive.

Suddenly people start shouting "*Krishnaparanth*!!" I look up and see two eagles right above the Sabarimala Sannidhanam. I am stunned and feel goose bumps on my arms. The two eagles are exactly above Sannidhanam, circling above the precious jewels, guarding them like protectors.

These unusual eagles are rarely seen where people congregate and, yet, these auspicious birds have followed the *Thiruvaabaranam* procession, finally circling above Sannidhanam at Sabarimala nine times as if paying their respects to the Lord.

During this time, there is not a single star in the sky except for a special Nakshatram. As the beautiful jewels are placed on the golden body of the Lord within the temple, the several hundred thousand devotees outside, who are crammed into any available free space, chant "*Swamiye Saranam Ayyappa*".

When the jewels have finally been placed on the idol, adorning the Lord, I experience a feeling of eternal bliss. Then, at around 6.50 p.m., a radiant brilliance appears three times on Ponnambalamedu the hill opposite Sabarimala. The *Makara Jyothi* is clearly seen by us all and there is not one person who is not affected by the sight. After five minutes, a small star is seen exactly above the Kaandamala Mountain. The star is shining brightly and emits various colours at one time.

Vaahanam: Vehicle.

Thiruvaabaranam: The jewels - ornaments, armour, etc – that will adorn the Lord Krishnaparanth: Holy Garuda eagles, considered the vehicle of Lord Vishnu.

Nakshatram: The holy star.

At 7.30 p.m., we start moving towards the temple for *Darshanam* of Lord Ayyappa. As we approach the temple, we can see that the flag stand above the sanctum-santorum is emitting a beam of light straight upwards.

When night falls upon Sabarimala, I stare at the slowly appearing stars until they completely fill the night sky. Despite the windy conditions and cold temperatures, I cannot tear myself away from the awe-inspiring beauty of the cosmos.

ACE *Insights* 7

Reflections On The Way To The Top: As I climb, I am always reminded that climbing a mountain is a metaphor for the journey of life. Even though I am focused on taking just one more step upwards, Neelimalai still affords me time to reflect on what has been happening to me as I climb.

Go slow to go fast: On the first few days of the trek, I wanted to blaze the trail ahead of the others. But the hills have taught me that to go slow is to go fast.

Twenty minutes into my Neelimalai trek, I know this is true. When I began, I had boundless energy. Now I am in agony, swaying and staggering with every laboured breath under the affects of altitude sickness.

Yet, slowly, at what seemed like a snail's pace, I do make it to the top of Neelimalai along with all the others.

Reflection: There are always areas in life where we need to slow down.

Be aware that the temptation to hurry and take short cuts will cost you in the long run.

Both the journey and the destination are important: There is a profound sense of accomplishment and exhilaration that we all feel when we make it to the top. But there is truth in the saying, "It's all about the journey, not the destination."

We need to take time, as we struggle towards our goals, to enjoy the landscape, nature and each other's company.

Reflection: As you strive to your ultimate goal, make sure you enjoy the moments of your life along the way.

Working hard to reach the top: As I climb, I am aware of all the long months of preparation, fasting, planning and dreaming of the ultimate goal of climbing to the summit. Now I am underway. Now I can taste the victory at the end and the fruit of all my labours.

Reflection: Set a goal, plan and prepare, and then work hard to achieve your dream. The hard work will be worth the effort. The pride you will feel when you reach your goal will be priceless.

It takes a team to live the dream: There are so many of us on this journey together and, as we all reach the Pamba base, we can rejoice together in each other's success. It is indeed a great thing.

In the last two days on my journey, I have had the chance to befriend many strangers from many different places like Malaysia and Australia who are now good friends. We have become a team and share the challenging Sabarimala journey together.

Reflection: Allow friends or family members who share your passions to pursue your dream with you.

Overcoming obstacles is part of pursuing any dream: Why am I investing all this time to inflict pain on myself by climbing a mountain?

Can I make it? Each time the trek becomes so tough that I think I cannot continue, these questions that I have suppressed resurface and tempt me to give up and turn back.

Reflection: We all face doubt whenever we are faced with opportunity or challenge that will require risk yet great reward on the other side.

The key is to be strong enough to suppress the doubt and persist with your dream – one small confident step at a time.

Celebrate your victories: It is hard to put into words the euphoria I feel when I get to the top of the mountain.

Perhaps it is simply the lack of oxygen that makes me feel a little light-headed, but I think it is also that sense of fulfillment, joy and feeling of being truly alive.

Even though I am bone weary, cold and plagued by the aches and pains of my efforts, the joy and exhilaration are overwhelming.

Even before I reach the summit technically, I am still truly elated and proud of myself and my accomplishment.

Reflection: Celebrate all the large and small accomplishments in your life and in the lives of those you care about. Celebration builds confidence in people and helps them to risk and face failure.

Cheer the next generation: As we get closer to finishing our trek, I see that there are still thousands of people attempting the climb. That's when I realize my bigger role. I need to be the cheerleader for the next generation, encouraging them to dream big and go for it.

Peak Point

Massive accomplishment leads to massive confidence.

Reflection: The next generation needs us as coaches and mentors. We must cheer them on and, when they ask, pass on our life wisdom.

More importantly, perhaps, we must create space for them to explore, risk, and, yes, sometimes fail. They need us to be the champions of their dreams.

MILESTONE

8

The Next Peak - Inspire the Next

"It is not the mountain we conquer but ourselves."

Sir Edmund Hillary

On January 15th, I wake at 2.30 a.m., bathe in the cold waters of the Bhasmakulam Pond and am among the first to pay my obeisance to the Lord when the temple opens at 4 a.m.

After I finish my prayers and have packed up all my belongings, I am ready at 7:30 a.m. to begin my descent to Pamba.

The descent is more enjoyable than the ascent, not only because there is less physical challenge but because I feel refreshed inside. I feel lighter because I have accomplished what I have come to achieve.

Now, as I walk down the Holy 18 Steps, I climb down each step with a sense of accomplishment, taking time to enjoy the natural world around me - the forest, the sounds of the animals, the high trees trying to touch the sky and the monkeys jumping from branch to branch.

It is indeed a fulfilling experience. When I reach Pamba, I take a dip in the holy river.

At about 9.30 a.m., I am back at the Kannimoola Ganapathy Temple. After a quick breakfast, I take the KSRTC bus that will bring me to Kottayam at 3:30 p.m.

I have lunch, rest, take some tea and then reach the Cochin Airport which will return me to Chennai. From there I will make my way home.

Home

The pilgrimage and sojourn to Sabarimala end only when the pilgrim returns home and removes his holy *Maalai*.

Bhasmakulam: The holy pond atop the Sabarimala hill.

Karpoora Aarathi: Paying obeisance by lighting camphors.

I do a *Karpoora Aarathi* and then take the *Prasadams* home. Only after this can I remove the M*aala*.

I return home fresh, spiritually content and rejuvenated after my journey. I have had a memorable

Darshan and my Sabarimala trip has taught me how to stay grounded and that the luxuries in life are not as important as the state of mind we are in.

Over the years, my pilgrimages have made me calmer and have improved my focus and concentration. They have helped bring balance into my life.

Apart from the trek itself, the satisfaction and sense of fulfillment I feel at the end of my journey is something that will keep me going for quite a while now.

By putting my true self to the test, the Sabarimala experience has allowed me to pull down all my pretences and elevate myself upon a pedestal. I can stand on higher ground after the emotional, physical and spiritual exertion and the triumph.

Whether one comes from privilege or poverty, from royalty or common birth, whether one is young or old, black or white, the Sabarimala trip is an equalizer for everyone. Each one of the pilgrims needs to start at ground zero, at the bottom, and be prepared to start fresh, no matter what their past credentials are, and be prepared to work hard in order to make their way up to the summit of the sacred mountain.

And so it is with me. After many adventures and detours, I discover that my old self has changed and I have to create my life all over again.

I thought the great reward for successfully making it to the peak would be seeing the beautiful view, something I never would see anywhere else in the world. But that was not all. The reward I truly valued most was conquering my fears and limitations and being molded by the experience of the physical climb itself.

The reward of reaching the peak is not as valuable as the changes the climb makes in my life.

I have learned that I am able to climb to the peaks of my own life and that I can smile through each day regardless of my circumstances.

But has my journey really ended?

No, I think not. In fact, I think my journey has truly just begun.

ACE *Insights*

8

Life Lessons Learned

Throughout my journey, I have learned something new each day.

If you truly want to succeed and experience true happiness, peace and a sense of accomplishment, as I do when I climb Sabarimala, you have to work hard and stay focused.

Life is full of crevasses, foot holds, steep ascends and sharp declines. There are always sharp edges and rough patches. But hidden opportunities lie among these dangers. How we make use of them and how we maneouver ourselves around them is what determines the extent of our successes or failures in life.

Although I may be prepared for the sheer amount of physical strength I will be required to display, I may not be prepared for the psychological and emotional exertion the journey requires. In fact, I have learned a lot about myself and what I am capable of throughout the journey. I have new respect for my inner strength.

A difficult journey in which we triumph can restore our faith in the goodness of people. Generally, people want to help and want us to succeed. Believe in people, they generally don't disappoint.

Success begins where our comfort zone ends. When I step outside my comfort zone, the things that make me uncomfortable are what teach me so much about myself.

As we negotiate our way through the difficulties of life, we need to look for supports, identify them, test them and use the tools and skills we have accumulated to accomplish our goals.

Every relationship, obstacle and goal looks like an impenetrable mountain at first. Our instincts and emotions can blind us and make us feel as if the task at hand is too much for us and we will not be able to achieve our dreams.

If we let negative thoughts rule our minds – cynicism, negativity, insecurity, anger and rage – we will surely not succeed. But, if we take a step back and develop a broader perspective of it all, we can learn to understand the obstacles for what they are and can have a clear mental picture of how to overcome them.

Most importantly, with the right preparation, knowledge and attitude, we can prepare ourselves and have a greater chance of succeeding.

It is important that we search for and identify new ways of dealing with our feelings which will become the boulders and hand grips that help us climb life's mountains. They will help us get ahead in life safely, quickly and on more secure footings.

When we learn to control our minds, our bodies follow

When the fasting season begins, from November to January, it is always toughest in the beginning. I cannot indulge in my favorite foods or gulp endless cups of coffee and tea. Suddenly, I have to deny myself almost everything. In the first 72 hours, my body begins to rebel.

But then, a miraculous thing happens. By day four, if I have persevered, my body responds and the fasting becomes easier from that day onwards.

In fact, by the end of the two-months fasting period, I am not yearning for my Teriyaki Experience and Honey Garlic Chicken. I do not really want that cup of tea or coffee anymore. The cravings are gone.

We may think we cannot live without the things that we have come to rely on in our lives. But we can. We only have to persevere and concentrate on our dreams of success. If we have passion, we can do it.

When I begin my trek, I must take off my comfortable shoes and force myself to walk barefoot through unpaved jungle paths and sleep on logs with a bare minimum of clothing on chilly nights.

The first three to four hours of the trek are the toughest. The climb appears steeper than it really is and the head gear I have been wearing for 26 years now seems heavier than I remember.

The truth is, my mind is looking for every possible excuse to make me give up, turn back and take the bus to Pamba.

But, if I can stay focused and in control on the first night on the trek, the rest of the 55 kilometres' climb is, in fact, actually easier.

The mind is a powerful thing and difficult to control. But it can be controlled. Learn to control your mind and your body will obey every instruction.

The tools that are the key to success

Relationships with others are very important in making a success of a mountain climb or a life's journey. Good deeds, acceptance and respect for others, decent behaviour, honesty and loyalty are the key tools I use to help me get through the tough patches on the mountain. They are the hooks and pulleys through which I can thread the ropes that will pull me up to the summit.

Relationships with close friends and family members are vital in life. As you reach out and grab on to the ropes when you climb, so relationships play a similar role in your life. Strong relationships help you get through your life's journeys because those around you that you can count on will help and support you. But you must cultivate these relationships and make sure the bonds you create with those you care about are strong and durable.

Service to others

Service is reciprocity.

When you are giving of yourself without expectations of some reward for doing it, it feels authentic and, both you and the other person are winners. When you devote yourself to serving others, you open yourself to be your best you.

Let service flow naturally, not because you must but because you want to. Your passion, knowledge and actions will show you the heights you can achieve.

What you can give to others

Time

Time is one of the most precious gifts you can give. It is altruistic because once you give it, you can never get it back.

Wisdom

Sharing your knowledge, positive experiences and spiritual testimonies with others is extremely important. It not only reminds you of your blessings and successes but it can also provide the much-needed hope that someone else has been seeking.

Compassion

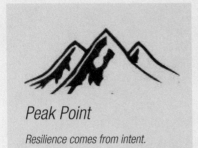

Peak Point

Resilience comes from intent.

Sometimes people do not need their problems solved for them but they do need someone to listen. When we have someone to talk to, it helps us sort things out in our minds. Often, just a hug or some other warm human contact can go a long way.

Resources

Whatever you have in abundance you can give to someone who has need.

A resource is anything that provides for a person's needs. This can be a a phone number to a local charity, a dollar, a blanket, a cup of water or a place to sleep.

*"Karmanye vadhikaraste ma phaleshu kadachna
Karmaphalehtur bhurma te sangostvakarmani"*

*"You have a right to perform your prescribed duty,
but you are not entitled to the fruits of action.*

*Never consider yourself the cause of the results of your activities,
and never be attached to not doing your duty"*

Ch. 2. 47, The Bhagavad Gita, the Holy Book of Hinduism

Summary

Now I bring you the torch to carry forward into your own life.

This is my gift to you and this book is dedicated to the climber and prevailer within you.

I hope, as you prepare to climb your own mountains, that you will cherish the experience and, by doing so, I assure you that you will begin to live with more happiness, accomplishment and success.

Let the Mountain of Experience take you to the peak of your life and set you on a path that many others can follow.

After climbing Sabarimala, there is one thing I know for sure. The experience is not about conquering the mountain, it is about conquering myself and the relationships I form in the process.

There is a reason why I continue my pilgrimage to Sabarimala each year without fail.

With each trip, I get to know the mountains and myself better and the experience just keeps becoming richer. After climbing Sabarimala, I can honestly say I am a better man. With each climb, each year, I am constantly being challenged to keep learning and overcoming my own limitations. I am striving to be a better version of myself.

As I write this book from my Markham home, bask in the warm sun and look back on the journey, all the special thoughts and feelings associated with the trek come flooding back.

I undertook the austerity, the discipline of fasting for two months and the rigours of the climb across five peaks and I have happily endured it so that I can experience the exhilaration of having risen to the top - feeling myself above the ordinary. That is why I am willing to push myself to do it again and again every year and in all the years to come.

I wish you the heights of success and happiness.

Murali Murthy

Appendix # 1

The 10 Best Treks In The World

What the Experts Recommend *(Courtesy: Lonely Planet)*

These 10 classic treks are for serious walkers. All of them require a sturdy pair of lungs, fit legs and a good amount of preparation. However, if you choose to go on any of these trails then you will be rewarded with experiences that last a lifetime. In no particular order:

1. GR20, France. – This demanding 15-day (168km, 104mi) slog through Corsica is legendary for the diversity of landscapes it traverses. There are forests, granite moonscapes, windswept craters, glacial lakes, torrents, peat bogs, maquis, snow-capped peaks, plains and névés (stretches of ice formed from snow). But it doesn't come easy: the path is rocky and sometimes steep, and includes rickety bridges and slippery rock faces – all part of the fun. Created in 1972, the GR20 links Calenzana, in the Balagne, with Conca, north of Porto Vecchio.

2. Inca Trail, Peru. – This 33km (20mi) ancient trail was laid by the Incas and is currently traversed by thousands each year. The trail leads from the Sacred Valley to Machu Picchu winding its way up and down and around the mountains, taking three high passes en route. Views of white-tipped mountains and high cloud forest combine with the magic of walking from one cliff-hugging ruin to the next – understandably making this South America's most famous trail.

3. Pays Dogon, Mali. – 'The land of the Dogon people' is one of Africa's most breathtaking regions. A trek here can last anywhere between two and 10 days, and takes in the soaring cliffs of the Bandiagara escarpment inlaid with old abandoned cliff dwellings. Dogon villages dot the cliffs and are an extraordinary highlight of the journey. The Dogon are known for their masked stilt dancers, intricately carved doors and pueblo-like dwellings built into the side of the escarpment.

4. Everest Base Camp, Nepal. – Reaching a height of 5,545m (18,193ft) at Kala Pattar, this three-week trek is extremely popular with those who want to be able to say, 'I've been to the base of the world's highest mountain'. The difficult trek passes undeniably spectacular scenery and is led by Sherpa people of the Solu Khumbu. The heights reached during this trek are literally dizzying until you acclimatize to the altitude, and the continuous cutting across valleys certainly has its ups and downs.

5. Indian Himalayas, India. – Fewer adventurers trek on the Indian side of the world's greatest mountain range. So, if isolation's your thing, try trekking in Himachal Pradesh. Hardcore hikers can try teetering along the mountain tops for 24 days from Spiti to Ladakh. This extremely remote and challenging walk follows ancient trade routes. The bleak high-altitude desert terrain inspired Rudyard Kipling to exclaim, 'Surely the gods live here; this is no place for men'.

6. Overland Track, Australia. – Tasmania's prehistoric-looking wilderness is most accessible on the 80km (50mi), five to six-day Overland Track. Snaking its way between Cradle Mountain and Lake St Clair (Australia's deepest natural freshwater lake), the well-defined path (parts on boardwalks) passes craggy mountains, beautiful lakes and tarns, extensive forests and moorlands. Those who want more can take numerous sidewalks leading to waterfalls, valleys and still more summits including Mt Ossa (1,617m, 5,305ft) – Tassie's highest.

7. Routeburn Track, New Zealand. – See the stunning subalpine scenery of New Zealand's South Island surrounding this medium three-day (32km, 20mi) track. At the base of New Zealand's Southern Alps, the track passes through two national parks: Fiordland and Mt Aspiring. Highlights include the views from Harris Saddle and atop Conical Hill – from where you can see waves breaking on the distant beach. The main challenge for this popular hike is actually securing a place among the limited numbers who are allowed on the track at any time.

8. The Narrows, USA. – A 26km (16mi) journey through dramatic canyons carved over centuries by the Virgin River, the Narrows in Zion National Park is a hike like no other. The route is the river, with over half of the hike spent wading and sometimes swimming. The hike can be traversed in a day, though some choose to take the hanging gardens and natural springs at a more leisurely pace – spending a night at one of the park's 12 camp grounds.

9. The Haute Route, France-Switzerland. – Leading from Chamonix in France through the southern Valais to Zermatt in Switzerland, the Haute Route traverses some of the highest and most scenic country accessible to walkers anywhere in the Alps. The summer Haute Route walk (which takes a different course than the more famous winter ski touring route) takes around two weeks to complete. It mainly involves 'pass hopping' and demands a high level of fitness, with every section containing a high huff factor.

10. Baltoro Glacier & K2, Pakistan. – This corridor of ice leads to the colossal peak of K2 (8,611m, 28,251ft), the world's second-highest peak. This incomparable trek traverses some of the most humbling scenery on the planet. What begins following icy rivers boldly goes to the guts of the glacier before leading to the granite pyramidal mountains including Paiju (6,610m, 21,686ft), Uli Biaho (6,417m, 21,053ft), Great Trango Tower (6,286m, 20,623ft) and ultimately K2. If the 15 days don't floor you, take side trips to more moraine-covered glaciers.

Appendix # 2

Top 10 Mountains To Climb In The World

What the Experts Recommend *(Courtesy: National Geographic)*

1. Mount Khuiten, Mongolia. – In Mongolia, it's easy for a traveler to be quickly swept away by the endless green steppes, the heartiness of the Kazakh nomads, and the rolling landscapes that define the Altai Mountains. This makes the trek to Mount Khuiten as enjoyable and scenic as the climb itself. The mountain straddles the corners of Russia, China, and Mongolia. To reach it, trekkers must cross a golden, vast, and barren landscape that is one of the last remote regions on Earth. This remarkable journey is enhanced by the gentle hospitality of the Kazakh nomads.

2. Kilimanjaro, Tanzania. – Flat-topped Kilimanjaro is Africa's highest mountain. Located on Tanzania's northern border with Kenya, the mountain is made up of three extinct volcanoes, Kibo, Mawenzi, and Shira. The highest peak, Uhuru, is 19,340 ft (5,899 m) high. Reaching the top of Kilimanjaro is exhilarating. Take the Machame Route up so you can see the region's wonderful animals and birds. Then you'll begin the trek across the Shira Plateau through the Grand Barranco Canyon and on to the top where you could reach Stella Point and continue around Kibo's rim to Uhuru.

3. The Andes, Peru. – The Inca Trail is an in-depth journey through a variety of ecosystems, from plains to desert to tropical cloud forests. You'll pass views of snowcapped mountains and rushing rivers. The highlight is Machu Picchu, the famed lost city of the Inca that was discovered in 1911 by Hiram Bingham. Then continue your trek to what was the heart and soul of the Inca Empire, Cusco.

4. Mount Everest, Nepal. – Rising 29,035 ft (8,856 m) above sea level, Everest is the highest mountain on Earth. For decades, reaching its top has been considered one of the greatest mountaineering achievements. Sir Edmund Hillary and Tensing Norgay accomplished this feat in 1953 when they approached the peak along the South Col route. Since then, more than 2,000 others have made ascents through South Col. It is, by far, the most successfully climbed route on the mountain.

5. The Matterhorn, Switzerland. – Nestled in the Swiss Alps, the Matterhorn is the most recognized mountain on the European continent. In the shape of a roughly chiseled rock pyramid, this peak serves as a defining geographical landmark. For many climbers, ascending the Matterhorn, the birthplace of the sport of mountaineering, represents a return to the purist traditions of climbing.

6. Mount Elbrus, Russia. – Dynamic in both region and terrain, Mount Elbrus stands as a watchtower in the Caucasus Mountains between Europe and Asia. Elbrus is a large, double-coned volcano, whose summits vary by about 65 ft (20 m). For the climber with moderate skills, the highest mountain in Europe has great appeal because it presents a strenuous, yet rewarding climb. The mountain's location affords visitors excellent opportunities to see the region's large melting pot of ethnic groups, such as Turkish, Georgian, Azeri and Russian.

7. Cilaltépetl and Iztaccíhuatl, Mexico. – In the heart of Mexico, about 800 mi (1,287 km) south of the United States border, Citlaltépetl and Iztaccíhuatl are the third and seventh highest mountains respectively in North America. The first is 18,406 ft (5,614 m) tall, while the second is 17,159 ft (5,233 m) tall. Ascents of these two volcanoes are by far the most attractive climbs in Mexico. From a distance, it's easy to see how Iztaccíhuatl or "white woman" got its name; the snowcapped peaks look like the head, breasts, and feet of a sleeping woman.

8. Denali, Alaska. – Mount McKinley, also called Denali in Athabascan. Located in Denali National Park, Alaska, at 20,320 ft (6,194 m), it is the highest mountain in North America. From its base to its apex, it rises nearly 18,000 ft (5,490 m), an elevation gain unsurpassed anywhere in the world. No other mountain offers such breathtaking and diverse views each day of an ascent. Its tremendous size and beauty create a magnetism that continually draws climbers from around the world. Choice months for attempting Denali are May and June, before the threats of avalanches and open crevasses become too severe. The mountain provides an unforgettable experience, touching the psyche of all mountaineers who have undertaken its challenges.

9. Annapurna, Nepal. – In terms of sheer geological and cultural diversity, a trek to Nepal's Annapurna region is unbeatable. By circumnavigating the giant Himalaya, you'll see everything from lush bamboo forests to arid high mountain landscapes. Most visitors here climb over the famous Thorung La (17,599 ft; 5,368 m). The hike into this glorious mountain pass rewards one with spectacular blazes of orange as the sun rises, casting the white Himalayan peaks in a fiery glow.

10. Damavand, Iran. – The Elburz Mountains stand huge and stunning as they lean against the Caspian Sea northeast of Tehran. Damavand's peaks range in altitude from 18,400 ft (5,612 m) to more than 19,000 ft (5,795 m). Steam rises from the hot springs and fumaroles that pockmark this dormant volcano, and two small glaciers provide dazzling views.

Glossary

Aazhi – Campfire.

Aarthi – Lamps lit in obeisance.

Abhishekham – Offering.

Appaachimedu – The hill found atop the Neelimalai, close to Sabarimala.

Annadhanam – Mass food offering to devotees and the needy.

Ayyappa Temple – The Ayyappa legend is famous in India for its shrine in the Sabarimala hills. Each year millions of people from around the world trek all the way up to the mountain to pay their obeisance in what has become the second largest pilgrimage phenomenon in the world.

Azhudha River – A tributary of the Pamba River, about 2 kilometres from Kalaketti. On the far side of the river is the steep Azhudha hill, famous for its arduous track.

Bhasmakulam – Holy Pond on Sabarimala.

Chinna Paadhai – The shorter route. It is the straight route from Pampa to Sabarimala.

Darshanam – Sighting, Viewing.

Deekhshaa – Holy Period of fasting.

Dharmasastha – Another name for Ayyappa.

Divya Jyothi – Divine Lights.

Erumeli – Small hamlet in Kottayam district and the starting point for the Sabarimala trek.

Rudraksha Malal Tulsi Mala – Beads worn around the neck.

Guru/Guruswamy – The mentor who plays a significant role in the Ayyappa legend. The whole concept of Sabarimala revolves around the Guruswamy.

Guruswamy Vaakyam Pramaanam – The Guruswamy's words are Final.

Inchipparakota – Important stop after Kallidum kunru enroute to Karimalai.

Irumudi – A cloth bag worn on the head by each pilgrim. It contains offering items such as coconuts, dry fruit, sandalwood paste and turmeric and meagre provisions for the pilgrim.

Kalasham – Crown above the temple.

Kallidum Kunru – Holy stop at the peak of Azhudha Hill.

Kanniswami – First time pilgrims to Sabarimala.

Kari – Elephant.

Karimalai – Probably the toughest mountain to climb. Its steep height is legendary and can overwhelm even seasoned climbers.

Kari Valam Thodu – The Karimalai canal, the base of Karimalai and the starting point of the Karimalai trek.

Karpoora – Camphor.

Kettu Nerai – The process of filling the Irumudi, the offerings bag. This can only be done by a qualified Guruswamy.

Kaalaketi – First stop 10 kilometres from Erumeli at the foothills of the Azhudha Mountain.

Kaandamala – A mountain to the east and exactly facing the main shrine on Sabarimala.

Makara Jyothi – Divine Lights.

Makara Sankranti – The 14th of January.

Margazhi – The 'holy months' of November and December when, for a minimum period of 41 days, the devotees fast and observe strict celibacy.

Maala Dharanam – The process of wearing the holy Maala – beads around the neck.

Mandala Vrutham – The duration of the fasting period.

Mukkuzhi – An important stop on the descent form Azhudha enroute to Karimalai.

Nadi – River.

Namasthe – The popular Hindu greeting performed all over India and by Indians all over the world. It is done by pressing two hands together and holding them near the heart. The act communicates to the world: "You and I are One. I salute and worship the God within you which is a mirror image of myself."

Nazhikkinar – At the Karimalai summit, a well within a well of fresh spring water.

Neelimalai – The first mountain on the banks of the Pampa en route to Sabarimala.

Nei or Ghee – Clarified butter.

Pathinettampadi – Holy 18 Steps.

Pamba River – The holy river on the banks of Sabarimala.

Peruvazhi – The longer trek route.

Peri Yaaynai Vattam – Base of Karimalai and camping grounds on the banks of the Pamba River.

Pettai Thullal – Traditional dance performed by devotees before embarking on the trek.

Pooja – Prayers.

Poongavanam – Holy gardens.

Pori – Rice flakes.

Perur Thodu – A river bank about 4 kilometres from Erumeli.

Prasadam – Holy offering.

Sabarimala – Sabarimala or Mount Sabari rises 3,000 feet above sea level and lies in the Sahyadris, the Western Ghats. It is the site of one of the largest annual pilgrimages in the world with an estimated 50–60 million devotees walking barefoot through forests abounding in wildlife. It is a spiritual journey that underscores universal brotherhood, regardless of caste and creed.

The Sabarimala temple is open to people from all castes, creeds, religions, social status or nationality. Today, the pilgrims comprise every religion, though mostly Hindus, Christians and Muslims.

Sadhya – Feast.

Saathwick – Vegan food in its pristine form.

Saranams – Holy chants of the Swamis on the trek.

Saram – A small arrow made of bamboo.

Shishyas – Disciples.

Shlokas – Hymns.

Siri Yaanai Vattam – A small meeting place for elephants and the starting point of the Karimalai descent. The path down is renowned for its boulders, rocks and huge trees.

Swami/Swamy – The term given to the devotee undertaking the trek to Sabarimala.

Swamiye Saranam Ayyappa – *"Lord, give me shelter, take me under your wings."*

Sannidhanam – The summit of Sabarimala.

Thiruvabharnam – Ornaments, armour, etc. used to adorn the Lord's idol at the summit of Sabarimala.

Thodu – Stream of Water.

Uchi – Peak.

Valam – Wander.

Vavar – Muslim warlord, loyal to Ayyappa, who has a shrine dedicate to him at Erumeli.

Vibhuthi – Holy ash, smeared on the forehead.

Vilakku - Lights.

Viri – Makeshift tent.

Virutham – The fasting process.

Vrutha Kaalam – The fasting duration.

Yatra – The journey.

Yendhividappa, Thookkividappa – Chants that mean: "God! Pick me up, lift me up."

Printed in Canada